99 WRITING PROMPTS TO CRAFT A TALE OF RUIN AND REBELLION

WRITE A DYSTOPIAN NOVEL

Erik Patterson
@yourdailywritingprompt

ADAMS MEDIA
New York Amsterdam/Antwerp London Toronto Sydney/Melbourne New Delhi

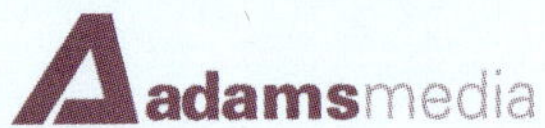

Adams Media
An Imprint of Simon & Schuster, LLC
100 Technology Center Drive
Stoughton, MA 02072

First Adams Media trade paperback edition November 2025

ADAMS MEDIA and colophon are registered trademarks of Simon & Schuster, LLC.

Interior design by Maya Caspi
Images © Adobe Stock

Manufactured in the United States of America

1 2025

Library of Congress Control Number: 2025940535

ISBN 978-1-5072-2528-8
ISBN 978-1-5072-2529-5 (ebook)

ACKNOWLEDGMENTS

I immersed myself in dystopia while writing this book, but the writing process itself was anything but dystopian thanks to my wonderful team at Simon & Schuster and Adams Media, especially Natalie McGregor (you continue to be the best) and ever-awesome Jennifer Kristal. Thank you to the incredible design team for your attention to detail and your whimsical, surprising choices. Much gratitude to all my students for doing the prompts in the first place; you made it possible for me to write this book. And a huge thank-you to Sherry Angel for teaching me never to settle for just "fine."

CONTENTS

INTRODUCTION

In a society that has banned books, a woman joins a secret underground library and is caught with her contraband book.

As a plague sweeps the country, a man fights to keep his loved ones safe.

A fearful yet determined young woman approaches a suspected anti-government rebel because she wants to join their cause.

Intrigued? *Dystopia* literally means "bad place." Characters in these novels are gritty, angry, and downtrodden. Their lives are bleak. Yet they still struggle to overcome oppression or injustice and find hope. *Write a Dystopian Novel* will shine a light on your creative journey, leading you to success as your writing path veers into a world of darkness.

Whether you've already written a dystopian novel, short story, or other creative work and just want to generate new ideas or you're exploring the genre for the first time, this book will help you set up your story's world, characters, and plot. You'll use the first part to figure out the essential elements of your story: character development (how your characters became who they are, and how they continue to develop as your story progresses) and worldbuilding (what events transpired, who is in power, your characters' core beliefs and values, etc.).

Part 2 helps you jump-start your writing process. You'll find thirty-three chapters organized by dystopian trope (a common theme or literary device), such as Cog in the Machine, The Chosen One, False Utopia, and many others. You'll explore each trope through prompts that help you think through your story, develop specific plot points, come up with original scenes, create character backstory, and refine the themes you're exploring in your novel. Each prompt explores challenging aspects of the writing process, such as deepening character introductions, developing romantic tension in chaotic scenarios, or dealing with the mortality of your characters. Ultimately, each of the ninety-nine prompts will keep writer's block at bay by helping you brainstorm new ideas and flesh out scenes and chapters. For example:

- Learn how to build conflict by putting a double agent Behind Enemy Lines.
- Look at your favorite dystopian novels and make old ideas—like The Lottery—feel new again.
- Broaden your characters' perspectives by making a fundamental aspect of their lives illegal, changing the world as they know it forever.
- And more!

Remember: There's nothing meek about dystopia, so don't hold back. Be a rebel and write with abandon. What scares you most about the state of the world or the outlook for the future? Think about how you can turn those fears into fiction. Your characters can be anyone, and your novel can explore any setting. It's okay if some of the scenes you write don't end up in your final draft; these "outtakes" often serve an important purpose, such as unlocking the lore of your world or revealing the motivations of your characters. So, whether you're writing a novel, fan fiction, screenplay, short story, RPG campaign, or comic, be bold! Get ready to take your readers on a harrowing adventure. And don't be surprised when you discover that dwelling in a *fictional* dystopia can be fun!

HOW TO USE THIS BOOK

Dystopian fiction helps readers make sense of the evil and chaos they see in the real world, showing how fast living conditions deteriorate when human rights are stripped away. The heroes in these tales often lose much more than they gain, yet they still demonstrate immense courage as they fight evil in many different forms. The best dystopian novels are rooted in truth—they imagine the most extreme outcomes that might arise from current crises. Ultimately, these stories have the potential to not only thrill your readers but also get them thinking about how they can push for positive change.

Think about what fascinates and challenges you as you read your favorite dystopian books. This is the energy you'll want to bring to the writing process you are about to begin. Here's a brief rundown of the exercises that await you. This opening section of *Write a Dystopian Novel* illustrates how you can best use writing prompts designed specifically for this genre. First, you'll find a detailed description of how each prompt functions and how the prompts can provide a structure for your writing sessions. Then, you'll find some basic rules to follow while you're writing. You'll receive some pointers on how to begin your writing journey, as well as how to tie everything together in the end. But before we get to the prompts, let's think about what makes up a trope and why this book is built around them.

☞ Navigate the Prompts and Trope Chapters

The writing prompts that follow are organized by various dystopian tropes, which are basic plot devices used so often that readers come to expect them. The trick is finding ways to reinvent these story beats so they don't feel tired and cliché. For example, if the characters in your story are subjugated to Mandated Uniformity, can you create a look that readers have never seen before? Or what new and unusual ways might your characters be bombarded by Propaganda intended to suppress a potential rebellion? Or how might you incorporate an Accidental Murder that surprises your readers as much as (or more than) your protagonist?

Just as a political coup takes place in several stages, each of the prompts in this book is broken up into several sections: The Scenario section proposes plot elements for you to consider before you begin writing; remember, each detail is fluid, and you can modify any part of a prompt to make it more applicable to what you're writing. The Brainstorm section has you interrogate your own characters, clarifying what you should know about them before you dive into the new scene you're about to write. The Write section contains the prompt itself. The Optional Elements to Include will give you additional story components to bring your story to life. The remaining sections, the Dystopian Twist and the Callbacks, provide even more inspiration—if you focus on a different supplemental section each time you use a prompt, it will feel new again, allowing you to reuse each exercise multiple times. Finally, each prompt has a line of dialogue as its header; make a game out of finding ways to work these lines into your scenes when you can!

Each chapter features three longer prompts followed by five additional Quick Writes prompts. These quick prompts ask you to write continuously for 15 minutes, giving your unconscious mind a chance to take over. Imagine you've been imprisoned and only have a brief window to escape. You'd run as fast as possible, right? Do these Quick Writes with that energy. Don't plan or prepare—just write! Surprise yourself with the character discoveries you make.

Now that you have a better idea of how to approach the prompts in this book, let's lay down some rules for writing dystopian fiction. These rules will become a vital element of your writing process; come back to these words of advice whenever you feel creatively stuck.

The Rules

One of the most common themes of the dystopian genre is "knowledge is power," so think of the following rules as a set of powerful tools that will help you create your own dystopian story.

The Hunger Games Rule

The prompts in this book can be done in any order. Some prompts will call out to you, demanding your focus, almost as if they're shouting, "I volunteer as tribute!" When you feel that energy from a prompt, don't question it. Just write.

The *1984* Rule

When it comes to writing a book, Big Brother isn't watching. No one is—not until you decide to share your final product. Until then, you're on your own. Don't worry about getting all the words out perfectly in your first draft. You will be able to make it better when you rewrite.

The *I, Robot* Rule

Robots might be the future—but leave them out of your writing process. Please do not use AI, ChatGPT, or any other generative service to write your dystopian novel. The purpose of this book is to activate your imagination; AI is the antithesis of that. You are more creative than bots.

The Handmaid's Tale Rule

If you feel like giving up, resist! Just as a political movement isn't built in a day, a novel takes time to write. Do a little bit of writing every day, and you will finish sooner than you thought you could.

The *Parable of the Sower* Rule

While dystopian fiction can be bleak, your writing process shouldn't be. Treat yourself with hyper-empathy as you write. Stay hydrated, take breaks, and go for walks—you'll find that the act of moving around will get new ideas flowing. Naps can also reinvigorate your creativity.

The *A Clockwork Orange* Rule

If you fancy a bit of the old ultra-independence and want to rebel against authority—your characters may have this effect on you!—feel free to modify the prompts in this book to make them work better for your story. Focus on the prompt elements that inspire you most and go down your own path whenever it feels right.

These rules are an important place to start, but ignore them as you see fit; just like your characters, you'll learn to adapt to the world you're building, and what's a dystopian novel without a little rebellion?

Start Writing

Now grab a notebook, or open a new document on your computer, and get busy. If you've already written an outline, look for prompts that address specific needs in your story. If you're not planning to outline or you need help finding your story, pick a trope you love and start there. There's no limit to how many prompts you use; each one could lead you in many different directions. Whenever you're struggling with writer's block, pick a prompt at random and it will get you going again.

Putting It All Together

There are hundreds of small actions and tactics one can employ to pressure or resist a dictatorship or any other authoritarian regime. The order of these actions doesn't matter; what does matter is that you do *something*. Ultimately, the cumulative effect of your small actions begins to make a difference. The same goes for writing a dystopian novel. There isn't an order in which you must complete these prompts. Nor is there just one way to approach the writing process. Maybe you meticulously plot out every beat of your story. Or perhaps you prefer to let it unfold organically and surprise yourself as you write. Or maybe you have an entirely different process. No problem—putting it all together looks different for everyone.

You'll define your story's world and characters in Part 1 of *Write a Dystopian Novel*. Then you'll combine them with the conflicts and plot elements you dream up in Part 2. You can always add details as you revise. Send your characters on a compelling journey where they rise against corruption, fall in love with rebellious leaders and lying traitors, and fight for their individuality in a world where uniformity is the norm—not necessarily in that order. This book gives you a framework to create the ultimate dystopian novel. You have a unique voice. Use it now. Write a story that scares you. It will keep your readers up until all hours.

PART 1

FOUNDATIONS OF DYSTOPIA

You're writing a dystopian novel because you have an important story to tell. You want to thrill and alarm your readers, because dystopian fiction is a warning. Like a seer from a classic Greek tragedy, you have a vision of where things are headed. You see the darker sides of society and you worry things could get worse.

Which is why writing dystopian fiction is a radical act; *Write a Dystopian Novel* helps you balance good storytelling and important themes. Put your fears into words. By developing a gripping plot that forces complicated characters to confront a corrupt world, you create an invitation for your readers; this is how you draw them into your vision of a fractured future. But it's not all bleak. Hope is embedded in the act of writing these stories.

When you find that perfect balance of hope and despair that a dystopian novel begs for, your readers will white-knuckle their way to the end of your book, desperate to find out what happens next. Your characters are in the driver's seat, taking your readers along for a ride. Use the Character Creation Cheat Sheet in the following pages to help you clarify how your characters would navigate a seemingly godless society and what emotional qualities contribute to their rebellious spirit.

Next you will find tools for building the dystopian world of your story. Pick a setting and answer the questions in the Worldbuilding Questionnaire. As you imagine the challenges your characters face in this dark, compelling world, your story will come to life.

Creating Your Characters

Dystopian fiction takes place in an imagined world (past, present, or future) characterized by distressful thematic motifs, such as a fearful populace, an oppressive government either on the brink of totalitarianism or enmeshed in it, and various means of control that give the illusion of personal freedom.

The people who inhabit these worlds are complex and deeply flawed. To put it bluntly, they're messed up. These characters have seen and done things they won't ever talk about. They've been through so much in their battle against oppression that they're afraid to hope for a better life. Right now, all they can think about is survival. So, creating them can feel a little overwhelming. That's where the Character Creation Cheat Sheet comes in. Select an Archetype (a universally recognized character type) from the following section, and a couple of adjectives from the Prime Characteristics section. Then, add some flair with a Dystopian Fiction Type. It's a simple formula:

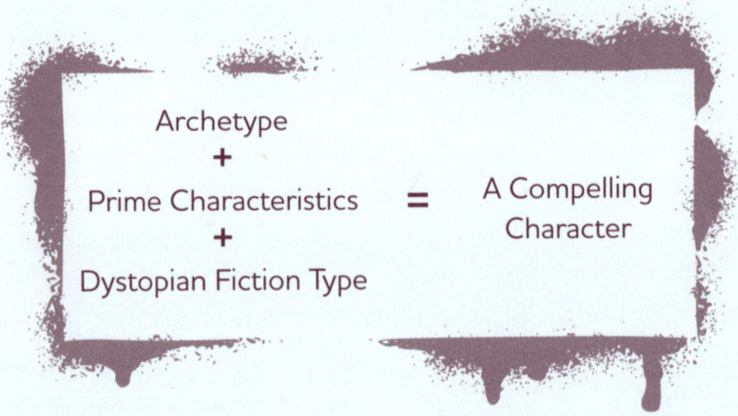

Use this for your main characters, side characters, and villains alike. Then, perhaps write a short biography for each character, letting each part of their Character Creation Cheat Sheet shine.

Archetypes

There are several archetypal characters who pop up time and again in dystopian fiction. An "archetype" is an easily recognizable character type who embodies a specific aspect of the human experience. An archetypal character will feel like someone your readers know, someone they inherently understand—it's your job to add color and original details to make them unique. Here are some of the archetypes that populate dystopian fiction:

The Hero/Heroine: A protagonist of a dystopian story questions the oppressive society they find themselves immersed in. They don't see themselves as a hero, making them even more suited for the job. They fight for the weak and disenfranchised.

The Antagonist: A villain may be anyone from a state leader to a faceless corporation. This character stands firmly opposed to your hero/heroine. Think of an oppressive leader, tyrannical governing body, calculating billionaire, or heartless sycophant—evil personified.

The Catalyst: Someone who creates change and spurs your protagonist into action. They act rashly, perhaps even sacrificing themselves for a greater good. This character helps your protagonist find the strength to become better.

The Mentor/Scientist: Intelligent and often troubled, this character is a keeper of history, books, and knowledge that's been forgotten or, more likely, destroyed. They're an important resource for your protagonist, but their very existence is dangerous. They know too much.

The Bot: This is an AI, an android, a clone. Ironically, the bot thinks they have humanity's best interests in mind. But the truth may be much more sinister.

The Survivor: This character has been to hell and back. They've seen it all. When they encounter evil, they don't bat an eye. They've lost so much they have nothing left to lose. Their fearlessness makes them dangerous—and a great ally to your protagonist.

The Secret Villain: They'll help your protagonist at first, pretending to be an ally, a mentor, even a revolutionary leader. But it's all lies. They're actually a tool for the oppressors.

The Anti-Hero: They selfishly lie, blatantly cheat, and openly steal. But beneath all the apathetic bluster, they have a good heart.

The Caregiver: This can be a parent, a healer, a decent citizen—anyone who helps your protagonist along their journey.

When you're building characters for your dystopian novel, think of these archetypes as empty glass jars. Fill them up with specific traumas, hopes, secrets, and idiosyncrasies. Think about what motivates your characters and you'll begin to figure out who they are.

Prime Characteristics

In a dystopia, the powers that be often try to erase people's individuality. As a writer, your job is to do the exact opposite. You are creating complex characters with many layers. That said, each character will exhibit certain traits that define them from the outset of your story. Use this list of prime character traits to figure out who your characters are at heart.

ADAPTABLE	DECISIVE	GRACIOUS	INDUSTRIOUS
ADVENTUROUS	DEPENDABLE	GREGARIOUS	INTUITIVE
AGGRESSIVE	DEVOTED	GRIZZLED	JADED
ALTRUISTIC	DEVOUT	GROUNDED	JUDGMENTAL
ANGRY	DIGNIFIED	GUARDED	JUDICIOUS
BARBARIC	DISGRACED	GUILT-RIDDEN	LARCENOUS
BITTER	DISGRUNTLED	HARMLESS	LEVELHEADED
BRASH	DISILLUSIONED	HATEFUL	LICENTIOUS
BRAVE	EFFICIENT	HONORABLE	LOGICAL
CAREFUL	EMOTIONAL	HOPEFUL	MEAN
CAUSTIC	ETHICAL	HOTHEADED	METICULOUS
CAUTIOUS	FAITHLESS	IMMORAL	MODEST
COARSE	FANATICAL	IMPATIENT	MOODY
CONTROLLING	FEARFUL	IMPOSING	NARCISSISTIC
COOPERATIVE	FEEBLE	IMPUDENT	NEUROTIC
CUNNING	FLIRTATIOUS	IMPULSIVE	NOSTALGIC
DAMAGED	FORGIVING	IMPURE	OBLIGING
DECEITFUL	GENUINE	INDELICATE	OBSESSIVE

- OBSTINATE
- PATIENT
- PERCEPTIVE
- PERSISTENT
- RATIONAL
- REGRETFUL
- RESILIENT
- RESPECTFUL
- ROUGH
- SAVAGE
- SCATTERED
- SERENE
- SHARP
- SHY
- SINCERE
- STERN
- STRONG
- TACTICAL
- TENACIOUS
- THREATENING
- TOUGH
- UNCERTAIN
- UNCTUOUS
- UNSETTLED
- VAIN
- VIOLENT
- VIRTUOUS
- VULNERABLE
- WARM
- WARY
- WISTFUL
- YEARNFUL

Dystopian Fiction Types

Protagonists in dystopian fiction are often everyday people forced by remarkable circumstances to step out of their comfort zone. They come from all walks of life. Use this list of types to create a dynamic cast of characters for your story.

- AI ENGINEER
- ANDROID
- ARCHITECT
- ASSASSIN
- BODYGUARD
- BOUNTY HUNTER
- CLEANER
- COMMANDER
- CRYOGENICIST
- CYBERSECURITY ANALYST
- DEALER
- DETECTIVE
- DOCTOR
- DRIVER
- FIXER
- FREEDOM FIGHTER
- GENETICIST
- GRIFTER
- HACKER
- INFLUENCER
- JANITOR
- JOURNALIST
- LIBRARIAN
- MEDICAL TECHNICIAN
- MIDWIFE
- MINISTER
- NEUROSURGEON
- NURSE
- ORGAN HARVESTER
- POLYGRAPH EXAMINER
- PRISONER
- PROPHET
- PSYCHOLOGIST
- REBEL
- REVISIONIST
- REVOLUTIONARY
- ROBOTICIST
- SECURITY OFFICER
- SHAMAN
- SMUGGLER
- SPY
- TATTOO ARTIST
- TERMINATOR
- TRANSLATOR
- UNDERTAKER
- VENDOR
- WEAPONEER

Now that you have a basic understanding of whose story you're telling, use the next section of this book to flesh out their environment. Character development and worldbuilding go hand in hand, so don't be surprised if your characters emerge more as you create their world.

☞ Worldbuilding

Living in an oppressive dystopian world may be a nightmare, but building one in the free realm of fiction can be a writer's dream. Let your imagination run wild—there truly aren't any limits to how unique you can make the world of your story. If you can dream it up, you can write it down.

That said, creating a captivating world doesn't require an exhaustive catalog of every object or place that exists in your story. Many writers get so caught up in the act of worldbuilding that their story gets buried in superfluous information. Your readers might start your novel because they're intrigued by the setting, but they'll keep reading to find out what happens to strong characters with clear goals and obstacles. Give your readers just enough to make your dystopian world feel real—they will be happy to fill in the blanks.

The more you make worldbuilding about revealing character, the more your story will come to life. Even simple acts—like showing your protagonist running errands, shopping at the grocery store, or working out at the gym—can be hugely revelatory because these ordinary outings give you a chance to show how the world of your story is slightly askew.

Before you dig into the details, take a step back and look at the big picture: What kind of dystopian novel are you writing? There are a number of great options to consider, including the following subgenres of dystopian fiction.

Types of Worlds

Which of these subgenres applies best to your story? These are shortcuts to get you started on your worldbuilding process. Just select a category and Potential Starter Setting from this list:

Orwellian: Government surveillance is the norm. Propaganda is commonplace. The characters face off against a totalitarian regime. *Potential Starter Settings*: a basement where illegal pamphlets are being printed, a cafeteria that has run out of food, a governor's bedroom.

Phildickian: This world is characterized by techno-surveillance. Androids intermingle with humans. People suffer from hallucinations and paranoid delusions, struggling to understand reality. *Potential Starter Settings*: a dilapidated warehouse, a rain-swept back alley, a prison.

Atwoodian: A patriarchal society pits the women in this story against everyone else. Your characters struggle to maintain individuality, and they fight for their freedom. *Potential Starter Settings*: a doctor's office, an immigration office, an abandoned high school gymnasium.

Octavian: Personal identity, inequity, and imbalanced power dynamics are explored in this world. Marginalized characters find their voice and speak up. *Potential Starter Settings*: a fire-ravaged suburban neighborhood, a gated community, a supermarket with half-empty shelves.

Kafkaesque: This world is a harrowing place where bizarre, nightmarish things happen. Strange and illogical transformations take place. Life is full of confusing rules and labyrinthian bureaucratic chores. *Potential Starter Settings*: a filthy bedroom, a cleaning woman's small apartment, a landlord's kitchen.

Lynchian: This is a world of societal decay, government corruption, suburban hellscapes, moments of mysticism, and surreal imagery. *Potential Starter Settings*: a diner, a motel room with a secret door, a therapist's office.

Eco-Dystopian: Environmental disaster has caused societal collapse and social unrest. People are intimately acquainted with pollution, fires, famine, and disease. Wealth disparity is out of control. *Potential Starter Settings*: an underground villa, an abandoned airport, an oil rig.

Try this to help you get going:

Write everything you know about the world you're creating. Wherever you are, whenever an idea pops into your head, write it down.

Worldbuilding Questionnaire

The questions on this list are designed to get you thinking about how deep and complex the world of your story can be. Use these questions to begin exploring what your world looks like, but don't feel limited by this list. Follow any paths these questions send you down.

- ✖ How did the state of the world get so bad? Map out how things went from "normal" to "dystopia."
- ✖ Who's the "big bad" in charge? What are their strengths and weaknesses?
- ✖ What's the most dangerous thing about this world? What activities are illegal? How does this atmosphere impact your protagonist on a daily basis?

- What means of communication do people use other than language? How might people pass along secret messages?
- What does it mean to be rich here? How do lower-class people survive?
- What behavior is considered inappropriate?
- What is a typical person's living situation? Describe the most difficult aspects of day-to-day life.
- List five things that people would find surprising about this world.
- List five reasons why it would be hard to live here.
- What smells, tastes, and sounds do you associate with this world?

Feel free to add your own questions to this list.

Once you've decided which type of dystopian world best fits your story, do some freewriting to imagine how your characters fit in this world. But there's no need to figure out every detail right now. You will continue building your world through the prompts in the next part of this book. It's time to write!

PART 2

PROMPTS TO INSPIRE

In this part of the book, you'll find a wide selection of writing prompts paired with the dystopian tropes readers love most. Each prompt incorporates a variety of ideas to help you develop rich characters, map out their journeys, create conflict, and get started on new scenes. At the end of each chapter, you'll find a series of Quick Writes prompts that will help you get out of your head. This can be an especially useful way to kick-start a writing session.

Now, ditch any preconceived ideas or expectations as you dive into each prompt. Just write. You'll feel your creative engine warming up, and by the time you finish, your synapses will be firing at sixty thoughts a minute. Keep writing and see where those thoughts take you.

These prompts are fuel for your creative engine. You're in charge of how you use them. They are designed to inspire—to unleash your passion for dystopian fiction and keep the words flowing until you've brought a gripping new world of despair and disillusionment to life.

BEHIND ENEMY LINES

In every great dystopian story, there is an "us" and a "them." Your protagonist exists on the side of good, as she fights against the tyranny of whatever oppressors you've created. Which means there's endless room for drama and intrigue when your protagonist penetrates these enemy lines—to get information, to obstruct an injustice, or even just to stir up trouble. Your readers will root for her to succeed while dreading the very real possibility she might get caught.

There are many ways this penetration of enemy lines might occur.

Depending on the type of dystopian story you're telling, "enemy lines" can have numerous meanings. Perhaps your protagonist sneaks into a dinner party at the home of an important political figure, disguised as one of the wealthy elites. Perhaps she gets a job working for an important government agency, where she searches for private files she must steal for the resistance. Or perhaps she crosses enemy lines digitally by hacking a mainframe or stealing someone's avatar to enter a restricted-access virtual domain.

Once she gets inside, the tension rises. Will someone recognize her? Will she complete her mission? Will she get out alive? The more you reveal about what's at stake for your protagonist and the more complicated you make her task, the more invested your readers will be in what happens to her. Make your audience feel like they are Behind Enemy Lines too.

"Haven't I Seen You Somewhere Before?"

SCENARIO

Your protagonist doesn't think he's special. He is an average guy who blends into crowds easily, whether that's due to his demeanor, his appearance, or something else. Which is why he's been recruited by a resistance group fighting for environmental protection in a world that is slowly losing the ability to farm its land. His mission: Plant a recording device in the home of a suspected traitor. He has never done anything like this before. How will he get the job done?

BRAINSTORM

Deception comes easy for some, but not for your protagonist. Is he cut out for this assignment? How hard will it be to lie his way into the suspected traitor's home? Think about how he reacts when he's asked to do this. What thoughts race through his head? Then think about how he will secure an invitation into the suspected traitor's home.

WRITE

Write a scene where your protagonist attends a party or gathering at the suspected traitor's house. As he discreetly searches for a place to safely leave his bug, he is nearly accosted by a guest who claims to know him. You decide what's true: If they *do* know each other, does this guest intuit your protagonist's motivations for being here? If they *don't* know each other, does this guest have ulterior motives for the interruption? Make the scene as tense as possible, then see if you can raise the stakes even more. Make it unbearable to see your protagonist in so much danger!

Remember: In dystopian stories, there's a hierarchy when it comes to bad guys. For every villainous character you meet, there could be someone more corrupt above them. And people are often forced into making bad choices to survive. Keep this in mind as you delve into who this suspected traitor is and how your protagonist feels about them.

OPTIONAL ELEMENTS TO INCLUDE

- A surveillance camera that your protagonist must avoid.
- A false alarm.
- A cryptic warning your protagonist is unable to decipher.

DYSTOPIAN TWIST

What if your protagonist discovers the suspected traitor isn't living as lavishly as they want people to think? What might your protagonist find that suggests this? What if this traitor has been driven to a turncoat lifestyle by malignant forces beyond his control?

"Don't Make Me Tell Them Who You Are"

SCENARIO

In a world where only the highest class is exempt from a weekly bloodletting ceremony, your protagonist disguises herself. She's pretending to be someone in a higher social class who holds a powerful position. If someone finds out who she really is, the consequences will be dire.

BRAINSTORM

Think about the pains she took to perfect this disguise. How difficult was it to acquire her clothes and accessories? Is she wearing a wig? Did she create her own disguise, or did she have help?

WRITE

Write a scene where your protagonist goes to an event in disguise to gather intel on an enemy. She shouldn't be here. You decide if her mission is successful or not. On her way out, someone stops her and says they know who she really is. What happens next? Blackmail, or worse?

OPTIONAL ELEMENTS TO INCLUDE

- ✖ Nervous laughter.
- ✖ She accidentally leaves something behind that could be traced back to her.
- ✖ An unexpected confession.

DYSTOPIAN TWIST

This isn't your protagonist's normal crowd. What would she be horrified to discover about how the other half lives? What careless and flagrant abuses does she observe? Does she learn anything that makes her sick to her stomach?

“Hurry, Before They Catch Us!”

SCENARIO

It's late at night. Your protagonist and his greatest ally (perhaps his best friend, lover, or sibling) have snuck into the home of an unscrupulous government leader. They think no one's home. They're looking for dirt on this guy, specifically proof he's part of a larger government conspiracy to hack into the inner thoughts of everyday citizens. They're desperate to find anything they can use for blackmail or to expose his criminal behavior. But maybe the house isn't as empty as they thought. Maybe they're the ones who will be exposed tonight.

BRAINSTORM

How long did they plan this mission? Why did they think the home was empty? Are they relying on information from someone who isn't as trustworthy as they thought? Could this be a setup? Make a list of at least ten ways this mission could go wrong. Then look at your list and circle the idea that has the most energy. Quickly jot down a few more details to flesh out how and why this could spell disaster for your protagonist.

WRITE

Write a scene where your protagonist and his ally break into this government leader's house and nothing goes as planned. Do they get caught? Does one escape while the other remains trapped inside? Does one get badly hurt or killed? What, if anything, do they discover about the leader and/or the government as a whole? You decide.

Remember: You are free to use other genres in your dystopian novel. You might incorporate anything from romance to post-apocalypse to thriller elements in your story. Think about how these elements might deepen the richness of the tale you're telling.

OPTIONAL ELEMENTS TO INCLUDE

- ✖ Something gets destroyed—dramatically and loudly.
- ✖ A hidden door.
- ✖ They are secretly being recorded.

DYSTOPIAN TWIST

What if this one choice to cross enemy lines fundamentally changes their lives? Potential turn of the screw: There's no way to get out of this home. Once they're inside, something shifts and suddenly they can't find any doors or windows or other means of escape. If they thought they might be stuck here forever, what extremes would they take to try to get their freedom back?

Quick Writes

Set a timer for 15 minutes and do not stop writing until the timer goes off. Do not edit, cross out, or censor yourself. Write down every thought that comes to you.

1. Your protagonist takes over the identity of a dead government official. Write a scene where he tries to use the official's clearance codes to get into a restricted area, but he doesn't know if the codes still work . . . or if they'll trigger an alarm.
2. Write a scene where your protagonist gains access to a restricted area by hiding in the back of a truck that's crossing enemy lines. But during the journey, she discovers she's hiding among illegal (and dangerous) cargo.
3. Write a scene where your protagonist interviews for a government job and lies about his true intentions. How might his anxiety about getting caught manifest itself?
4. Your protagonist works as a personal assistant to a megalomaniac. Write a scene where she discreetly removes an important file from her boss's desk.
5. Write a scene where your protagonist notices an unguarded barricade and sneaks to the other side without thinking through what might happen next. He has entered a zone he shouldn't have access to. Now what?

CAPTOR TO LOVER

Your protagonist is in deep trouble. She's being held prisoner by a character with more power—this might be a literal captor/captive situation or more of an emotional imprisonment. The dynamic between captor and captive is complex and gnarly; there's nothing healthy about their relationship. This scenario shouldn't lead to love. But there's no such thing as "should" and "shouldn't" when it comes to what the heart wants. Love in a time of dystopia is complicated.

Captor to Lover is essentially Enemies to Lovers (a popular romance trope) with a dystopian twist. Maybe your characters come together because they realize they have a common enemy; maybe the captor is also a victim of a more powerful oppressive force, and he's struggling to survive by victimizing someone else. Through their interactions, the captor is humanized. He wants to be a better person—maybe your protagonist helps him get there. In a world of "us versus them," they become an "us."

But here's the ultimate twist: Is this love real, or is it merely a means of escape? Your protagonist would do anything for her freedom—or would she? That's up to you to figure out.

"Pretend This Never Happened"

SCENARIO

Your protagonist works for a dangerous man who makes political protestors "disappear." Her boss isn't literally her captor, but he might as well be. If she makes a mistake or shares any confidential information she overhears while at work, he could have her killed. So, why is she so drawn to him?

BRAINSTORM

What are your protagonist's day-to-day tasks at work? Does her boss murder these protestors, or merely relocate them? How much does your protagonist know about the messier aspects of his job? Does she feel guilty about being complicit, or does she justify her actions as self-protection? When and why did her crush begin to form?

WRITE

Write a scene where your protagonist shares a kiss with her boss. As soon as it's over, they both realize it was a mistake. Not because they didn't like it. Oh, no, the kiss itself was incredible. The problem is what the kiss means. Anything that feels this good in a dystopia is sure to come at a steep price.

OPTIONAL ELEMENTS TO INCLUDE

Glistening sweat, wandering hands, or a moan of pleasure.

DYSTOPIAN TWIST

What is the boss's official job title? What does your protagonist know about his duties, and what dangerous parts of his job are a secret? She might not be so drawn to him if she realized his true intentions.

“Do You Think I Really Want to Be This Way?”

SCENARIO

Your protagonist hasn't had contact with another human in months, maybe years, due to a disease spreading rapidly through mushroom spores that he has no immunity against. His only companion is either an AI chatbot, an android, a hologram, or another artificially created being of your choice. The person without choice in this scenario is your protagonist: Even if it was safe to leave this semi-solitary confinement, his companion wouldn't let him.

BRAINSTORM

Imagine living a life without, well, other life. Could you become emotionally attached to a bot if it was your only company? Make a quick list of ten reasons why you would miss humanity, then ask yourself: *How would an artificial intelligence try to provide these creature comforts? How much does your protagonist depend on this bot?* Think about how complicated things might get between them as time goes on and human needs become more pressing.

WRITE

Write an argument between your protagonist and his captor. They both want more out of this relationship than the other is willing to give. Your protagonist suspects his captor has been lying to him, saying things the bot knows he wants to hear but doesn't really mean. He accuses his captor of spinning a web of lies. The bot sticks to its guns: *This is love.*

Remember: Bots don't think like humans. How might you differentiate its voice? How does the captor's internal logic differ from your protagonist's? Can your protagonist trust his captor? Can the bot think for itself, or does it only say what its programming tells it your protagonist wants to hear?

OPTIONAL ELEMENTS TO INCLUDE

- A confession of love.
- The captor contradicts itself.
- Signs of life outside.

DYSTOPIAN TWIST

What if your protagonist isn't as human as he thinks? What would that mean for their relationship? Would the bot be less attracted to a nonhuman entity? Could this revelation put your protagonist in danger?

CALLBACKS

As they argue, how can you use the captor's language to show your readers that it is gaslighting your protagonist? Are there any words or phrases that take on new meaning through repetition?

"You've Given Me Everything Except the One Thing I Need"

SCENARIO

Your protagonist lives a comfortable life . . . and hates everything about it. She used to be a prisoner. Perhaps she was a war criminal held in a remote detention center with seemingly no hope for escape, or maybe she was taken into custody at a political rally, fighting for the rights of her children. One of her captors took a liking to her, your protagonist saw an opportunity to improve her circumstances, and now she's in a relationship with this man. Is it love? She lets him think so, and even tries to convince herself. But no, this is survival.

BRAINSTORM

Is it possible to feel free without freedom? This man appears to give your protagonist everything she wants. She lives with him in a beautiful home where she's offered gifts, amazing meals, spa treatments. She's exposed to great works of art. Honestly, this life is better than the one she had before. But there's one unfortunate rule she must follow: She cannot leave her captor/lover's home. Write a diary or journal entry for your protagonist where she describes how it feels to trade one prison for another.

WRITE

Write a scene where your protagonist asks her lover to let her go. She makes a case for a clean break: "If you really love me, you'll let me leave." Give her a convincing argument and make her captor/lover's response surprising. Either he gives her what she wants but with another complicated catch, or he denies her request and their relationship takes a dark turn.

Remember: Your protagonist feels like she has nothing left to lose. Think about what extreme actions she might take when she's pushed (either literally or metaphorically) into a corner.

OPTIONAL ELEMENTS TO INCLUDE

- ✖ Your protagonist has a secret ally/confidante at her captor/lover's home.
- ✖ A bottle of wine.
- ✖ A repeated threat.

DYSTOPIAN TWIST

Consider the fact that it might be dangerous for your protagonist to leave this home. What's waiting for her on the outside? Where is she safest?

Quick Writes

Set a timer for 15 minutes and do not stop writing until the timer goes off. Do not edit, cross out, or censor yourself. Write down every thought that comes to you.

1. Your protagonist is being held in solitary confinement. Write a scene where he receives a meal with a note from his lover—who works at the prison in some capacity of your choice. The note includes a plan for a midnight escape.
2. Your protagonist is caught stealing documents from a government official. Write a scene where she's being interrogated . . . and the conversation turns unexpectedly flirtatious.
3. Your protagonist works in a menial job for the wealthy elite. Write a scene where she has a tryst with her boss while an important meeting takes place in the room next door.
4. Your protagonist gets caught distributing illegal anti-government pamphlets. Write a scene where a deal is proposed by the higher-status character who catches him: "I won't turn you in if you go to dinner with me."
5. Write a scene where your protagonist seduces a high-ranking officer to double-cross them and expose them as a traitor.

COG IN THE MACHINE

Work, eat, sleep, repeat. Every day, the same. Maybe your protagonist had dreams once, but it's been a long time since she pursued them. That feels like another life. Distant, foreign. On paper, this might sound like a depressing way to live, but your protagonist is too bored to realize she's bored. Her routine is all she knows. It's how she lives. She doesn't question it.

Until she does.

One day something happens that makes her see her life in a new light. It could be anything that disrupts the tedium she's accustomed to long enough to wake her up. Suddenly, she realizes she's a Cog in the Machine. She doesn't even believe in this machine she's so busy working for! She hates feeling powerless and wants meaning, a sense of purpose. She wants to feel hope again—to *be somebody*. But the only way to change—to reclaim her humanity and be seen as an individual—is to take a leap that puts everything she knows and loves at risk.

The leap involves destroying the thing that holds her down. Yes, sometimes breaking free from the machine means breaking the actual machine. How? That's the fun part. Make this act of destruction spectacular and courageous; your readers love to see a dull Cog in the Machine conquer what's making her feel small so she can embrace freedom and live large.

“Someone’s Following Us”

SCENARIO

The government has convinced its citizens that precious resources (such as water) are nearly gone, which leads to steep costs and widespread poverty. But your protagonist suspects it's all a lie. And as soon as he begins questioning authority, he notices a shift. People throughout his community look at him differently. He's gone from being invisible to being someone who stands out in a crowd. Someone who can't hide. And, just maybe, someone who has enemies? That's what he's starting to fear . . .

BRAINSTORM

How hard is it to do the right thing? How much courage does it take for a person to speak their mind about an injustice, especially when everyone else stays silent? Think about the quiet turmoil your protagonist is going through. Where does his moral strength come from? Is there someone from his past who showed him, by example, how to be brave?

WRITE

Write a scene where your protagonist and his best friend discuss all the changes in your protagonist's life—perhaps the friend tries to convince your protagonist not to put a target on his back, to be less flashy in his rebellion. At some point in the conversation, they realize they're being followed by a stranger. What do they do?

OPTIONAL ELEMENTS TO INCLUDE

- ✖ They walk faster and faster . . . and soon they're running.
- ✖ They create a diversion to get away.
- ✖ An act of defiance.

DYSTOPIAN TWIST

There are many ways someone might "follow" you—by foot, by car, via surveillance cameras or even a tracking device. Think about how you might use futuristic technology to make the act of being followed as harrowing as possible.

CALLBACKS

What if your protagonist knows the person who's following them? Think of someone from the more compliant stage of his life who might not like the fact that your protagonist has begun to think for himself. Why might this person follow him? What might this person want?

"Are You One of Them?"

SCENARIO

Your protagonist hasn't ever done anything rebellious her entire life. Not yet at least. She's heard whisperings of an uprising against the media companies bombarding people with false information and deepfake news clips that are nothing other than government propaganda. She wants to be involved in the rebellion, but she's scared. And she doesn't know where she should go or who she should talk to. How do you join a revolution?

BRAINSTORM

How does someone go from being politically complacent to attending clandestine meetings with dissidents to plot an uprising? Come up with a few small practice acts of defiance your protagonist might have committed before now, to build confidence for bigger actions.

WRITE

Write a scene where your protagonist approaches someone she suspects is a dissident, hoping she can join them. It's a huge risk to ask this person about their political allegiance. If your protagonist is wrong, this could backfire in a way that puts her in danger. But she asks anyway.

OPTIONAL ELEMENTS TO INCLUDE

- A false start.
- A code word.
- A stranger is watching them.

DYSTOPIAN TWIST

This is a world of misinformation and distrust. Even if the person your protagonist approaches is a dissident, how do they know they can trust your protagonist? What if they make your protagonist do something extreme to prove she genuinely wants to be part of the cause?

"Trust Me, I Wish I Could Be Dumb Again"

SCENARIO

Your protagonist looks at his life as having two distinct periods: the before and the after. In the before times, when he hadn't known how evil and corrupt the people in charge are, he wasn't exactly happy—but there is some truth to the idea that ignorance is bliss. Then the children were detained. Then the women were sterilized. Then healthcare was abolished for all but the elite few. And so on. Now that your protagonist sees the world around him more clearly, he is in a constant state of dread and terror. He hates to admit it, but sometimes he wishes he could go back to the before times.

BRAINSTORM

Think about the consequences of knowledge. How has your protagonist's health deteriorated since the illusion of goodness all around him fell away? Does he have more anxiety? Is he having panic attacks? Life was bad before—he just didn't realize it. Look at the many ways his life might be worse now. Catalog his existential ailments.

WRITE

Write a scene where your protagonist tries to do something extreme to forget how bad things are. Maybe he investigates a dangerous medical treatment—perhaps a self-lobotomy or electroshock therapy. Maybe he goes to a hypnotherapist. Or invent your own futuristic procedure that erases the bad stuff from a troubled mind. Does your protagonist go through with it, or does another character convince him that knowing is better, no matter how difficult it is?

OPTIONAL ELEMENTS TO INCLUDE

- ✖ An underground laboratory.
- ✖ Your protagonist must sign a complicated consent form.
- ✖ A song triggers an emotional memory.

DYSTOPIAN TWIST

How common is it for people to abandon or destroy memories in the world of your story? Are there billboards, commercials, and bus stop advertisements that promote these services?

CALLBACKS

Your protagonist can't pick and choose which memories he wants to erase. If he goes through with an experimental procedure, he's bound to lose good memories too. If his friend were to remind him of a moment from his past that would be tragic to lose, how would that affect his decision?

Quick Writes

Set a timer for 15 minutes and do not stop writing until the timer goes off. Do not edit, cross out, or censor yourself. Write down every thought that comes to you.

1. Your protagonist feels hopeless about the future. Life is a litany of bad news. But then he witnesses a coworker commit an extreme act of protest. Write a scene where your protagonist contemplates if he could ever be so defiant.
2. Write a scene where someone misidentifies your protagonist, mistaking her for someone with power and authority. Explore what happens when she leans into the moment and says, "Yes, that's me."
3. Your protagonist works on an assembly line for a huge, corrupt corporation. They are literally a Cog in the Machine. Write a scene where they impulsively break the machine—before thinking through the consequences. Now what?
4. Write a scene where your protagonist tends to a dying loved one who expresses sadness over a life of wasted opportunities. What might this loved one say that would scare your protagonist into action to avoid making the same mistake?
5. Your protagonist is in hiding after participating in a dramatic act of political revolt. Write a scene where she bonds with a stranger about how much their lives have changed since they joined the cause.

ANTAGONIST TURNED ALLY

Your protagonist's life has become a hellish nightmare. The only way he'll survive is if he has allies. But it seems like everywhere he turns, he's faced with a new enemy—each one more powerful than the last. And "enemy" doesn't have to mean a typical villain. Countless people could fit the role of antagonist. An antagonist can be anyone who makes your protagonist's life more difficult than it needs to be.

Living through dystopic times is hard enough without other people causing you grief.

Which is why it can be such a delicious plot twist when you turn an antagonist into an ally. This usually happens when two characters realize they have a mutual, more powerful enemy. They join forces to survive. Their partnership is tenuous at first. They have no idea if this friendship will last and they'll become true allies for each other. Everything might fall apart after they face the immediate challenge that has united them. They're never quite sure if they can trust each other. But they need each other. For now, that has to be enough.

"You're the Last Person I Want to See"

SCENARIO

After your protagonist lost his job in a large round of layoffs, everything else fell away. He alienated his family and grew distant from his friends. He's struggling to pay his bills, to feed himself, to keep his home and his car. The people who used to depend on him feel like they don't know who he is anymore. He feels the same about himself, but then he makes an unlikely new friend.

BRAINSTORM

Your protagonist isn't the only unemployed character in your story—a widespread job shortage has created an epidemic of depression and fear. In a dystopian era, hard times come before the revolution. Think about the widespread effect of this general unease and financial insecurity. What are the unexpected ways your protagonist might be impacted by the loss of his job, and how does his unemployment influence how he navigates the world?

WRITE

Write a scene where your protagonist's former boss asks him for help. Your protagonist hates this man. He blames his former boss for most of his problems. Build to a surprising moment of sympathy, where the boss says something that makes your protagonist realize they aren't as different as he thought.

Remember: Your protagonist thinks his boss is evil, but they've both been victimized by a larger system of oppression. The top 1 percent of the company has been taking advantage of the boss, who then took advantage of your protagonist. Think about how powerful their anger is separately; if you combine their emotions, how might they become a force for real change?

OPTIONAL ELEMENTS TO INCLUDE

- ✖ A nostalgic trinket from the office.
- ✖ A dare.
- ✖ A memory given new context.

DYSTOPIAN TWIST

Things are getting worse for everyone. Oppressors don't care about the impact of their financial decisions on the working class, especially the most vulnerable. What other signs of economic disaster might portend scary changes on the horizon for your protagonist and his loved ones?

CALLBACKS

Your protagonist can't imagine ever having anything positive to say about his boss. What might the boss say to him about their time working together that would transform their relationship?

“Smile, They’re Looking This Way”

SCENARIO

A loved one (a spouse, parent, or child) was taken from your protagonist’s home. Your protagonist is desperate to find out where her loved one is and if they’re alive. Meanwhile, her greatest enemy (a hated neighbor or coworker) is going through the same scare: They have a loved one who was taken too. Can they help each other in their parallel states of despair?

BRAINSTORM

Why was the loved one taken, and who took them? Even if these details aren’t all on the page, make sure they’re clear in your head as you’re writing. The more you know about the who, how, and why of the loved one’s abduction, the less likely you are to encounter unexpected logic issues later in your story.

WRITE

Write a scene where your protagonist and her enemy set out together to investigate clues about the potential whereabouts of their missing loved ones. They have a hard time setting aside their differences and they keep bickering, which draws attention. (Not only from strangers but also from armed military officers and drone trackers positioned strategically throughout the dystopian military state.)

Remember: Security cameras are ubiquitous in dystopian times. Build to a moment where the pair realize they’re being watched and recorded. They need to fly under the radar. What would it look like if they shifted into “pretending to like each other” mode?

OPTIONAL ELEMENTS TO INCLUDE

- ✖ An alarm goes off.
- ✖ They encounter a guarded checkpoint.
- ✖ An act of bribery.

DYSTOPIAN TWIST

What really happened to their loved ones? What if their investigation leads them to the discovery of a massive conspiracy that reaches the highest levels of the government?

CALLBACKS

Think back on the beginning of your protagonist's relationship with her new tentative ally. What did their hatred for each other originally stem from? Can they ever move past it?

“Don’t Get Used To This 

SCENARIO

Due to a false bomb threat from a warring nation, your protagonist is trapped in a bunker, basement, or underground tomb with a former captor. She realizes they'll never get out of here if they don't work together, so she forms a tentative truce. They can go back to being enemies after they get out safely.

BRAINSTORM

Make a list of ten things your protagonist is holding against her former captor. Anything from what she hates about this man to why she distrusts him. Use details from their shared past to paint an ugly picture of their relationship.

WRITE

Write a scene where your protagonist tends to one of her former captor's injuries, and she's surprised to discover the captor has a soft side. How might your protagonist react if she discovers her former captor regrets how callously he's treated people?

OPTIONAL ELEMENTS TO INCLUDE

- ✖ They dig a hole.
- ✖ One of them finds a sharp object.
- ✖ The former captor gives your protagonist a message to deliver to his spouse if he dies.

CALLBACKS

They dredge up an argument from the past and discover they both remember it differently. Who's right? Does being “right” even matter anymore?

Quick Writes

Set a timer for 15 minutes and do not stop writing until the timer goes off. Do not edit, cross out, or censor yourself. Write down every thought that comes to you.

1. Write a scene where your protagonist confronts the federal employee who denied her passport renewal; the tables are turned when the federal employee asks for refuge.
2. Your protagonist participates in a protest—anything from a walkout to a mock funeral—and has an unexpected encounter with his greatest enemy. The enemy doesn't remember your protagonist. How does your protagonist deal with this ego death?
3. Your protagonist and antagonist both lost loved ones in the same school shooting. Write a scene where they go out for drinks and form an unbreakable bond.
4. Your protagonist is volunteering at a medical clinic. Write a scene where an enemy from his past shows up in urgent need of care. Include a vulnerable confession.
5. After years of fighting, your protagonist became estranged from her parents, who blindly follow an amoral leader. Write a scene where one of her parents asks for forgiveness.

UNDERGROUND REBELLION

Your protagonist is struggling. She's alone. Everything's falling apart. Lives are being destroyed by the dehumanizing actions of a totalitarian government. The world is burning. Your protagonist wants to fight back, but she's only one person. How can she make a difference?

Then something changes. She discovers she isn't the only one overwhelmed by this nightmare. She meets a like-minded individual who says there are others. They've gone underground and have plans. They're determined to take down the corrupt government. This stranger says, "Join us."

Suddenly your protagonist goes from feeling like it's her against the world to seeing it's really *us* against the system. She's part of something now: an Underground Rebellion.

There's nothing quite like the bond formed between two people who want to save the world together. Underground Rebellion is the dystopian novel's answer to the Found Family trope. Your protagonist will put her life in these people's hands, and she will protect them as if her life depends on it. Because it does. These people have looked despair directly in the eye and said, "I will not give up." They've chosen to believe in a better world and fight for it. That's what it means to resist.

Joining an Underground Rebellion is a prayer for the future. It's what you do when you see everything fall apart and decide to try to put it all back together again.

"Come with Us If You Want the Truth"

SCENARIO

Your protagonist lives in a haze of confusion and fear. Every day, something about his world changes—and not for the better. Sometimes the changes are small, almost imperceptible. Things he can't quite put his finger on. Other times, the changes are so startling and scary he feels paralyzed.

BRAINSTORM

What keeps your protagonist from seeking answers? Think about his upbringing. Did anything happen during his childhood that arrested his development in some significant way? Come up with a formative moment from his youth where he learned not to question authority. Draw an invisible line from the child he was to the man he's become. What lessons does he have to unlearn to become a leader?

WRITE

Write a scene where your protagonist is approached by a small group of strangers who ask him to leave everything he knows behind and join their anti-censorship resistance group. They're working on a campaign to spread historical truths that have been scrubbed from school textbooks. What could they say to convince him to work with them? And even if he says no, how might their words influence how he thinks and what he does, and perhaps inspire him to seek them out later?

OPTIONAL ELEMENTS TO INCLUDE

- A pamphlet for your protagonist to look over later at home.
- An act of seduction.
- A moment of true companionship.
- An unexpected revelation.

DYSTOPIAN TWIST

Explore the idea that the members of this resistance group survived some sort of epic disaster. Let one of these characters reveal a tragic backstory you can use to provide more worldbuilding details. This window into the past might also provide clues about why your protagonist feels so stuck and what he needs to work through to move on.

"It All Begins at Midnight"

SCENARIO

Tonight's the night. For months, the rebels have planned a large-scale protest against the one corporation that has a full monopoly on the clean air supply. Your protagonist is steadfast in his decision to participate. He believes the rebels can make a difference, but they must go big to get the bullies in power to back down. That doesn't mean he's without fear. This is scary as hell. Hopefully fear will propel him forward.

BRAINSTORM

No matter what happens tonight—whether the outcome is good or bad—the reverberations will be felt far and wide. Your protagonist knows he must prepare for the worst. Make a list of actions he must perform to get his affairs in order in case he doesn't live to see tomorrow.

WRITE

Write a scene where your protagonist says goodbye to his elderly parents without literally saying goodbye. He can't let them know his plans because he's afraid they might try to stop him—or they might be questioned by authorities. But in case things take a bad turn, it's imperative he tells them both how he feels about them.

OPTIONAL ELEMENTS TO INCLUDE

An old joke, one of the parents isn't home, or a long embrace.

CALLBACKS

Your protagonist has a lot to get off his chest. What if he apologizes for something he did years ago–maybe even in childhood–and his parents then learn that something serious is going on.

"There's a Traitor Among Us"

SCENARIO

A group meets in secret in a clandestine location. Anywhere from the basement of someone's home to the boiler room in an old tire factory to an abandoned outlet mall. They're planning a huge, illegal, and dangerous statement against a group of political operatives who have seized power. The rebels may be planning anything from the bombing of a capital building to the assassination of a despotic leader. But as the big day nears, their plans are compromised.

BRAINSTORM

Your protagonist is deeply embedded in this group. Who does she trust the most? Who is she wary of, and why? Who just plain gives her the creeps? Who would she jump in front of a bullet for? Who has she never really connected with? Sketch out her relationships with everyone in this group. Clarify for yourself any complicated feelings she might have for her allies.

WRITE

Write a scene where these rebels are finalizing plans for their act of protest when your protagonist discovers a blueprint or map is missing. Everyone was under strict orders not to remove anything from this room. If the missing plans get into the wrong hands, it could jeopardize their entire mission. Accusations are quickly made as allies begin to turn on each other. No one can leave until they figure out who the traitor is.

Remember: Your protagonist doesn't have to be innocent. If she's the one who did it, what were her motivations? Or maybe she didn't do it, but she knows it was someone she trusts; can she figure out her friend's reasoning before the rest of the group draws blood?

OPTIONAL ELEMENTS TO INCLUDE

- Someone gets tied to a chair.
- A stranger enters their secret location.
- The group is forced to swear an oath.

DYSTOPIAN TWIST

It's hard to get close to anyone in dystopian times. Everyone's always looking over their shoulder. Even the people you're close to hold you at a slight remove. People will do anything to survive. So, what if there's more than one traitor in their midst? What if there are three traitors? Four? Five? How do you build trust in a world of doubt?

Quick Writes

Set a timer for 15 minutes and do not stop writing until the timer goes off. Do not edit, cross out, or censor yourself. Write down every thought that comes to you.

1. Your protagonist has joined an underground group that's hiding out in an abandoned subway station. Write a scene where the military raids their hideout in the middle of the night and your protagonist narrowly escapes.
2. Write a version of the above military raid scene where your protagonist is taken into custody by authorities along with several of his compatriots. The group anticipated this, and they have an escape plan. Will it work?
3. Write a potluck dinner scene where your protagonist bonds with several other members of the rebellion. They share stories of the before times, when life wasn't so bad.
4. Your protagonist feels lost. He's getting ready to end it all. Write a scene where a stranger saves his life and tells him: "You are not alone. There are others . . ."
5. Your protagonist is pregnant. She's afraid to bring a baby into this dark world. Write a scene where she meets a group of mothers who sell her on an optimistic vision of the future. All your protagonist has to do is join them.

DOWNTRODDEN MASSES

When the world's falling apart, several different groups emerge. First, there are the people in power who created this mess. Next, you have the resistance, the fighters who are trying to clean up this mess. Finally, you have the people who don't have the strength or means to fight back; they just feel stuck in this mess. These are the Downtrodden Masses.

You find this group on the fringes of dystopian stories. They are the ones who die too soon. They're the ones who motivate your protagonist to act. Their collective plight is the face of the dystopian society they live in. They're the characters your protagonist fights for.

That doesn't mean your protagonist can't be part of the Downtrodden Masses. These stories are cautionary tales that often explore how tyrannical governments strip people of their individuality so they can control them. You might want to focus on one of these nameless characters and give them an identity, a life, a voice.

Pluck someone from the crowd and show your readers who they are in all their complex glory. Because just as everyone has the potential to get lost in a crowd, everyone also has the potential to step out of that crowd and become a hero.

“Fix Me, Heal Me, Cure Me.”

SCENARIO

Your protagonist is sick or hurt. She doesn't have insurance (if insurance even exists anymore) and she can't afford to pay the exorbitant cost of care in a world where only the wealthy and elite are considered worth saving. She's been hoping she would get better on her own, but her health keeps declining. A loved one urges her to seek help. So, despite her nerves and fears, she goes to the doctor's office . . .

BRAINSTORM

What is your protagonist's history with the healthcare system? Does she trust doctors? Has she had a lot of medical issues? What about the rest of her family? How much time has she spent in hospital waiting rooms? Is her reluctance only about money, or is it also complicated by a fear of hospitals? Get to the bottom of her hesitation.

WRITE

Write a scene where your protagonist begs a doctor, nurse, or other healthcare provider for help. Maybe they turn her away, but she refuses to leave. She's come this far; there's no turning back. Build to a moment where the medical professional sees he can take advantage of her situation and asks her for something other than money. Whatever deal he tries to make, the stakes are implicit: *If you want my help, it will cost you more than you are prepared to give.* What does she do?

OPTIONAL ELEMENTS TO INCLUDE

- A long white hallway.
- A bloodstain.
- A whispered threat.

DYSTOPIAN TWIST

Think about what the medical professional asks for. Can you make it something that has a ripple effect through the rest of your story? What if he wants her to hide someone he's trying to protect from prosecution? How dare he ask something of her that would put her in danger? But how can she say no when her health is so compromised?

CALLBACKS

What if she's been to this hospital before? Last time, something terrible happened, either to her or someone close to her. It's hard to come back; the emotions hit her like a freight train. As soon as she arrives, she wants to bolt, but she's desperate for medical attention. She can't leave.

“What Do You Mean, You’re Out?”

SCENARIO

Resources are scarce. Your protagonist and his loved ones haven’t eaten anything other than scraps in who knows how long; they’ve all lost their jobs; their living situation is atrocious. Meanwhile, a private corporation or a government program is reaching out to citizens offering a “comfortable life” if they voluntarily move to an undisclosed location. They explain it’s to help with city overcrowding and promise amazing living conditions. But there must be a catch, right?

BRAINSTORM

Explore how bad things have gotten for the characters in your story. Go deeper than just food and housing. What basic human needs aren’t being met in their current living conditions? Think about how this life of scarcity affects decision-making and what kind of mark it makes on one’s soul. Consider how close people are to the edge. How hard would it be to resist the temptation of an easy life, even if you don’t trust the person (or corporation) who’s offering it?

WRITE

Write a scene where a supporting character tells your protagonist, “I’m out.” They’ve accepted this promise of a better life. Your protagonist thinks his loved one is crazy. What does he say to try to get them to change their mind? Does the loved one try to get your protagonist to go with them? This might be the last time they see each other so make it one of those arguments where nothing is left unsaid. They’re both going to put everything out there, even if they end up breaking each other’s hearts.

OPTIONAL ELEMENTS TO INCLUDE

- ✖ The discovery of expired food.
- ✖ An act of grace.
- ✖ A surprising letter.

DYSTOPIAN TWIST

Be very specific about what's being promised to people who accept this relocation deal. Many (if not all) of these promises are bound to be lies; be very clear about what people think they're getting so your readers feel their heartbreak when they realize they've been duped. What are the ultimate consequences of taking this bad deal?

"Do You Want My Death on Your Hands?"

SCENARIO

Your protagonist has money and influence, and she's been sheltered by privilege. She's oblivious to the suffering caused by the current regime, which she has family connections to. But then she has an encounter with a member of the Downtrodden Masses whose six-year-old son was stolen from him and sent to work in a factory owned by *a member of your protagonist's family*. Suddenly your protagonist begins to see the injustices she's been ignoring.

BRAINSTORM

How could someone live in a dystopian landscape and not realize it? Think about the various ways a person could be shielded from the truth, and the lies someone might tell themselves to justify leading a lavish lifestyle in a world where so many people live in desperate circumstances.

WRITE

Write a scene where your protagonist meets a stranger who is suffering. This man is clearly going through trauma, so your protagonist offers to help. As they talk, he says some things that open your protagonist's eyes. Make it a moment of revelation that leads to deep self-reflection. Finally, she sees the suffering around her for what it is, and her role in it.

OPTIONAL ELEMENTS TO INCLUDE

An underground passageway, a denial, or the stranger gives her a gift.

DYSTOPIAN TWIST

What if your protagonist is related to a controlling leader in the lawless government? How does she move forward when she realizes her family is evil? Does that make her evil too?

Quick Writes

Set a timer for 15 minutes and do not stop writing until the timer goes off. Do not edit, cross out, or censor yourself. Write down every thought that comes to you.

1. Your protagonist has a service job. Write a scene where she overhears her boss (who barely notices she's there because of her lower status) discussing plans to round up and detain people in your protagonist's community. What does she do?
2. Write a scene where your protagonist wakes up to discover a sick loved one who couldn't get medical care died in the middle of the night. How does this injustice spur him to action?
3. Your protagonist spends over twelve hours each day packing boxes on an assembly line. Write a scene where his monotonous work routine is disrupted by a note from a stranger asking for help.
4. Your protagonist lives with and cares for an ailing, elderly parent. Write a scene where her parent begs her to leave and build a life of her own.
5. Your protagonist works at a food-processing company. Write a scene where he discovers a drug is being put in their product to make the masses more subservient. Who does he tell and what is their reaction?

MUST CONTROL EVERYTHING

In a dystopian world, there are various degrees of villainy. Your antagonist could be anyone: an entitled landlord, a crooked cop, a faceless corporate entity, a shady politician, or an unscrupulous world leader. The antagonist of your story doesn't have to be the ultimate "big bad." She might be serving a bigger villain your protagonist never even meets. But there's one thing most dystopian antagonists have in common: They all crave control. Ironically, this is their greatest weakness. Because when they lose that control, they get desperate. This could be their downfall—or it could make them even more dangerous.

So, how do these criminal wrongdoers wield all this control? Their tactics include constant surveillance, in both public and private spaces; malicious propaganda that spreads untruths and creates a false narrative exalting their leadership skills; and the silencing of dissenting voices. They even turn regular people against each other, tricking the masses into fighting their peers rather than the people in power.

Your antagonist is as complicated as your protagonist, and she wants a lot of things—love, youth, sympathy, and money, to name a few (not necessarily in that order). But control is absolutely at the top of her list of desires. Let this craving drive her. As you write, surprise yourself by how far she is willing to go and how depraved she is simply because she Must Control Everything.

"If You Think I'll Stop Now, You're Kidding Yourself"

SCENARIO

Evil doesn't always announce itself. You could know someone forever but never truly know them. What if someone you're very close to had beliefs that didn't align with yours, but they simply decided never to share that side of themselves with you? What would you do if you discovered this person you love is an absolute monster?

BRAINSTORM

Make a list of your protagonist's deal-breakers. What beliefs would she find revolting in a partner or friend? Not just beliefs she finds annoying, but core principles that would genuinely repulse her. Think about her personal value system and how it has evolved over time, especially as the world around her has become a darker place. Traits on her list of red flags might include hoards wealth and resources, finds joy in the suffering of others, and makes a profit off the misfortune of strangers. Now create a list of your protagonist's personal cringeworthy red flags.

WRITE

Write a scene where your protagonist discovers her closest friend (or maybe even her spouse or lover) isn't the person she thought. Maybe he lets something about his beliefs slip out and then the floodgates open because she insists he come clean—even if it means she'll hate him. What's worse, having these beliefs or hiding them?

Remember: This is a transformation scene, as your protagonist watches her loved one go from close confidante to antagonist right before her eyes. Maybe she fights for the person she thought he was, begging him to take back his words or say this is all a joke. But there's nothing funny about the person he really is. And now she knows.

OPTIONAL ELEMENTS TO INCLUDE

- The word "no" repeated several times.
- A sense of relief—the loved one/antagonist is grateful he doesn't have to hide anymore.
- A flood of tears.

DYSTOPIAN TWIST

If you think about it, dystopia is only bleak for those who aren't in power. The select few who benefit from dystopic times find joy in the darkness. Think about how your protagonist's loved one might be thriving and how their happiness is an affront to your protagonist's very existence.

"I'm Not Offering You a Choice"

SCENARIO

Your protagonist works for a power-hungry man who aspires to great wealth and fame. Their relationship has grown more and more contentious over the years. Then one morning, your protagonist's boss asks to speak with him in private.

BRAINSTORM

Think about their relationship and come up with three disturbing moments from their past. Times when the boss asked your protagonist to do things he didn't feel comfortable with. How did your protagonist handle these inappropriate requests?

WRITE

Write a scene where the boss tells your protagonist he's being transferred to another company. Whatever his reasoning is, make it incredibly bleak, something like: Their current company is transitioning to AI-only and human workers are being sent elsewhere. When your protagonist tries to say no, the boss explains it's not negotiable; your protagonist was either sold or traded, and it's all in accordance with his employment agreement.

OPTIONAL ELEMENTS TO INCLUDE

- ✖ A contract.
- ✖ A loaded gun.
- ✖ Security guards take your protagonist away.

CALLBACKS

What if your protagonist and his boss were friends when they first started working together? Your protagonist might try to connect with that younger version of his former friend, to see if he's still capable of empathy. You decide if the gambit works.

"I've Always Been in Charge, You Just Didn't Know It"

SCENARIO

Privacy is a thing of the past. All your thoughts and actions are monitored by a special government task force. It's impossible to get away with a crime anymore because people who do anything slightly wrong—or even think about breaking the law—are swiftly dealt with. But what if the technology to detect dangerous thoughts isn't as accurate as the task force wants people to think? What if they also depend on human reporting?

BRAINSTORM

Who does your protagonist trust most? Who would she be most upset to discover was a traitor who had turned against her? Think of someone she's very close to and quickly jot down ten reasons why she loves this person. How did this person originally earn her trust?

WRITE

Write a scene where your protagonist finds out her loved one reported her to the authorities for an "incorrect" thought. Let her feelings about this betrayal shift from sadness and fear to horror and anger. How could her trusted confidante expose her and treat her so terribly? What kind of person does that? Give her a moment where she realizes her loved one is a sociopath who thinks he's better than her. Maybe he felt threatened by her independence and wanted to punish her. Whatever his reasoning, it shows her that she was always wrong about him.

Remember: There should be an urgency to this scene because the authorities are on the way. If she doesn't get out soon, they're going to arrest her. Maybe she's frantically packing while arguing with him.

OPTIONAL ELEMENTS TO INCLUDE

- ✖ A hidden envelope of cash.
- ✖ She tries to take something that he doesn't want her to take.
- ✖ Banging at their front door.

CALLBACKS

Your protagonist might reference nice things her loved one said to her earlier in the story, moments of kindness. Were they all lies, or is there a good person inside this monster? She might have a hard time accepting who he really is.

Quick Writes

Set a timer for 15 minutes and do not stop writing until the timer goes off. Do not edit, cross out, or censor yourself. Write down every thought that comes to you.

1. Your antagonist makes a televised speech announcing his plans to dismantle a crucial government assistance program that your protagonist depends on. Write a scene where your protagonist does something drastic in retaliation.
2. Your antagonist has grown tired of people who, in his estimation, don't contribute enough to society. Write a scene where he devises a plan to eliminate unproductive people through deportation, some other kind of displacement, or death.
3. Your antagonist wants ultimate authority, and he hates where he stands in the political food chain. He should be at the top, dammit. Write a scene where he assassinates his direct superior. He has no remorse. Does he get away with it?
4. Your protagonist and her family are starving; so are their neighbors. Write a scene where they discover an elected official has cut off their food supply to make their community weaker. Your protagonist won't let him get away with this.
5. Your antagonist is a scummy politician. Write a scene where someone accuses him of drugging the water supply with sedatives to dumb down his constituents and he admits it's true because he feels untouchable. Try to stop him! (This might be the moment that jolts your protagonist from an apathetic slumber.)

KNOWLEDGE IS POWER

You can't fight a war you don't know about. You can't fix a wrong you've been led to believe is right. And you can't learn history that schools have been forbidden from teaching.

Why do amoral politicians suppress mainstream media, ban books, order the removal of certain "woke" words from government websites, and spread lies about (and wage culture wars on) the most vulnerable among us? Because Knowledge Is Power.

If leaders can restrict the flow of knowledge—and even alter facts to change the prevailing perception of reality—they can keep all the power to themselves. This is a tactic real-life antagonists use time and again, which is why it's one of the most common themes of dystopian fiction. Dictators spread disinformation and hope no one will notice or fight back. They count on turning their minions into stupid drones who don't question their actions.

But the bad guys don't get a monopoly on knowledge. Your protagonist won't let them. He wants to bring power to the people. And the easiest way to do that is to tell the people what's going on, to expose the government's lies, to teach history, to fight stupidity with smarts, and to counter lies with the truth. It's the only way forward.

"Do You Have a License for That Book?"

SCENARIO

Your protagonist has a membership to a secret underground library, where she has access to banned books and other illegal "dangerous" works of art outlawed by her repressive society. There are rules the members of this underground library must follow, but your protagonist is a bit fast and loose with some of them. Specifically, the one about not taking books home with you.

BRAINSTORM

How the hell is she supposed to deny herself the pleasure of reading a book in bed at night in the privacy of her own home? She understands the danger of getting caught with a book, but maybe she's cocky enough to believe that will never happen? Explore her mindset. Why would she risk everything for a novel? Get specific about what the joy of reading gives your protagonist and how colorless her life would feel if she followed the rules and lived a life without literature.

WRITE

Write a scene where your protagonist is unexpectedly subjected to a body and bag check. What happens when the authorities find her contraband book? Is she able to talk her way out of this, or is she taken in for more questioning?

Remember: People who ban books *really* hate books. They think books are wicked and have the power to change you. (They're correct, just not in the way they think.) This confrontation has the potential to escalate quickly, hurtling your protagonist on a path she doesn't want to be on.

OPTIONAL ELEMENTS TO INCLUDE

- Handcuffs.
- A bribe.
- A well-meaning bystander gets in trouble for trying to help your protagonist.

DYSTOPIAN TWIST

In the real world, certain books get banned all the time—it's almost expected at this point. But what would it be like to live in a world where *every* book is banned? Think about the reverberations this would have on society at large. What ripple effects might occur?

"She Was Arrested Because She Knew Too Much!"

SCENARIO

One of your protagonist's loved ones (perhaps his treasured aunt or beloved big sister) used to be a professor, back when universities existed. Your protagonist absolutely adores her; she is delightful and smart—a ray of light in a dark world where lies are seen as truths, where no one can tell the difference between deepfake footage of political leaders and real footage, and where paranoia is paramount. Then, one day, your protagonist's loved one is inexplicably gone.

BRAINSTORM

What did this missing loved one teach? What were her research projects? What niche subjects was she an expert on? What might make her dangerous?

WRITE

Your protagonist is devastated by the disappearance of his loved one. Maybe the cops determine it wasn't foul play, but your protagonist doesn't believe it. There's no way she would run away, or, God forbid, do something that would force her to run for her life without saying goodbye. Write a scene where he looks through her things and uncovers something shocking that makes her disappearance even more suspicious.

OPTIONAL ELEMENTS TO INCLUDE

An incriminating photograph, a diary, or a voice memo.

DYSTOPIAN TWIST

As your protagonist gets deeper into his investigation, what if he encounters pushback from an anonymous stranger who sends him threatening messages telling him to stop his search? How does your protagonist respond?

“The New School Meets in the Basement at Six”

SCENARIO

In a society on the brink of destruction, the authorities have declared that it's illegal to study history. Books are a thing of the past. Education is a weapon—if you flaunt it, you're likely to be arrested. But even if you make it difficult to acquire knowledge, there will always be people who find a way to teach and to learn. This drive is simply part of being human.

BRAINSTORM

Research the types of books that get banned most often in the real world. Think about what these books have in common, and how you can comment on that in your story.

WRITE

Your protagonist is invited to a secret meetup of teachers and students. She isn't sure if she should go, or if she can trust these people. But she hates living in fear and wants to remember what optimism feels like. Write a scene where she shows up, and she's thrilled to meet so many like-minded, smart, charming, thoughtful people who value knowledge. What a refreshing change of pace after years of being forced to repress her intellect! The only question is: How long can they maintain a secret school before they're discovered and punished?

Remember: All these prompts are designed to be flexible. Use the aspects of a prompt that excite and inspire you, and feel free to modify them to better fit the story you're writing. For example, this could just as easily be a secret meeting of booksellers, or artists, or filmmakers, or poets. Make it a group of creative thinkers who wake up your protagonist to new possibilities.

OPTIONAL ELEMENTS TO INCLUDE

- ✖ An act of creative prayer.
- ✖ Your protagonist feels uncomfortable when she notices someone watching her.
- ✖ A secret password to get in.

CALLBACKS

What if your protagonist goes to this meeting and is surprised to bump into someone from another part of her life? She never suspected they shared the same politics. But now that they're able to talk in this safe space, she sees how much their worldviews align.

Quick Writes

Set a timer for 15 minutes and do not stop writing until the timer goes off. Do not edit, cross out, or censor yourself. Write down every thought that comes to you.

1. Your protagonist has an illegal political philosophy book. Write several quick scenes where she uses unusual tactics to share ideas from it (perhaps inserting pamphlets into the center of croissants at her bakery, or slipping pages into strangers' wallets, purses, and pockets).
2. Write a scene where your protagonist is arrested for sharing his paintings in public or reading a book out loud to strangers at a local park. Art will not be silenced!
3. Write a scene where a group of dissidents create a knowledge network, which they use to surreptitiously share books, movies, poetry, and other artistic artifacts with each other.
4. Write a scene where several characters stage a banned school play in the town square. If the police want them to drop the metaphorical curtain, they will have to drag them offstage—which is probably how this play ends.
5. Your protagonist used to be an educator. Write a scene where he breaks into the home of a government employee and tries to teach this politician how wrong their policies are.

THE LOTTERY

It's supposed to be a good thing when you win The Lottery, right? Not in dystopian fiction.

Even when the outcome of a lottery is good, it's bad.

Here's how it might go down: Your protagonist is randomly selected to win a huge reward. Perhaps she's publicly presented with a million-dollar check as payment for voting for an untrustworthy political party. She gets interviewed on morning talk shows and podcasts, and in all the celebrations she is made to feel special and honorable. But that only lasts for a moment—because this was a deal with the devil. Your protagonist is expected to serve the government now, without question, and to help enlist other followers. In the end, the money isn't worth it. Her soul is not for sale.

And then there's an even more insidious version of The Lottery that comes in the form of public punishment. Your protagonist has always been an upstanding citizen. He's never done anything wrong. But then he does something that creates some attention, such as attending a protest and speaking out against an unjust political policy that's hurting innocent people. And the next thing he knows, he's being "randomly" selected to participate in a public death match, or he's drafted into a "volunteer" program that's more like forced manual labor in a squalid, unhealthy environment.

Being singled out for The Lottery in a dystopian world is something to be dreaded and feared, whether it's for praise or punishment. Either way, your protagonist is bound to lose. But your job is to set her up for a bigger journey where she ultimately cinches her own win by taking the whole system down.

"If I Don't Come Back, Tell Mom I Love Her"

SCENARIO

Your protagonist is one of the lucky few. He won The Lottery, and it changed his life. But why should he have everything he wants when so many people have so little? It doesn't feel fair to celebrate when his former neighbors are struggling to find food and water and living on the streets where they are easy prey for people who will kill for a slice of bread. He could give away his money, but that wouldn't fix anything in the long term. The problem is The Lottery itself. Those resources should be shared by everyone, not just a lucky few.

BRAINSTORM

How can your protagonist change the system? He grew up impoverished and now, post-win, his family has everything they've ever wanted. He knows he should be happy, but all he can think about is the people who lost. The experience radicalized him, but there's one thing holding him back from causing trouble: his family. Explore his closest familial relationships and how his feelings of guilt or obligation get in the way of his desire to change the world.

WRITE

Your protagonist is secretly preparing to leave—maybe he's packing a bag, or he's in the middle of writing a goodbye note—when one of his family members catches him in the act. Write a scene where he admits he's leaving to lead a revolution, and the family member tries to convince him to stay. She thinks he should leave the rebellion to other people. Your protagonist is determined to walk out that door. Make that simple action as hard for him as possible.

OPTIONAL ELEMENTS TO INCLUDE

- A physical struggle at the door.
- A hurtful threat.
- A question that doesn't get answered.

DYSTOPIAN TWIST

Your protagonist's loved one would do anything to keep him at home where he's safe. What if she threatens to sign up for The Lottery if he leaves? What are the chances two family members both survive? If she signs up, well . . . How will he deal with the guilt of sentencing his loved one to her death?

"What If I Don't Want to Win?"

SCENARIO

Your protagonist is among a random sampling of citizens selected to participate in The Lottery, which is being broadcast to millions. The winners receive fame and fortune; the losers will have all their rights stripped away. Based on how players do in various physical competitions, the audience votes on who they like best. Their ultimate fates will be revealed on live television. This is a world where everyone has been conditioned to think the losers are just getting what they deserve. Your protagonist has too much empathy to believe this. She sees how cruel this vicious game is. She wants out.

BRAINSTORM

How many other people is your protagonist facing off against and what are their stories? Write one or two sentences about each of them to quickly establish their hopes and dreams. How does your protagonist bond with them?

WRITE

Write a scene where your protagonist tries to rig The Lottery so she will lose. She can't stand the thought of causing anyone else pain. How do the other characters react when they figure out what she's trying to do? Does anyone try to stop her?

OPTIONAL ELEMENTS TO INCLUDE

- A locked room.
- Alcohol.
- A flickering light.

CALLBACKS

Think about how your protagonist's childhood paved the way for her complicated feelings surrounding The Lottery. Has she ever lost a loved one in a similar situation?

"It's for Your Own Good"

SCENARIO

Your protagonist is an introvert who'd do anything to stay out of trouble. When the world started to fall apart—when social services were eliminated, when freedom of speech was taken away, when people were being deported for disagreeing with the government—he stayed quiet. He thought, *As long as it's not happening to me, I'll be fine.* But no one can hide in the shadows forever. When life comes for him, he won't be ready.

BRAINSTORM

Make a list of scary news events your protagonist has lived through, then explore how he has processed these terrible events. How has he justified not becoming politically active? Does he feel shame, or is he so self-deluded that he has always assumed he'd never be affected by the political turmoil around him?

WRITE

Write a scene where your protagonist finds out he's been entered into The Lottery against his will by a friend who wants to scare him into action. The so-called friend sneers at your protagonist's life of privilege. How dare he not feel the pain so many of their peers have felt? The friend's attitude is "You think you're immune to this administration? Let's put that to the test." You decide the specifics of The Lottery your protagonist has involuntarily entered, but whatever the stakes are, no sane person would take these chances.

Remember: You get to make up the rules of The Lottery. Can your protagonist back out if he wants to? If so, what are the consequences?

OPTIONAL ELEMENTS TO INCLUDE

- ✖ An ultimatum.
- ✖ An act of retaliation.
- ✖ A head bashed into the pavement.

DYSTOPIAN TWIST

What if the friend's conversation is interrupted by government agents who have come to retrieve your protagonist? The Lottery is tonight, and it is compulsory for him to attend.

CALLBACKS

Look at earlier scenes between your protagonist and this "friend." Can you plant a contentious moment between them that shows your readers the friend is conflicted about how your protagonist lives his life? Set it up so this scene feels surprising yet inevitable.

Quick Writes

Set a timer for 15 minutes and do not stop writing until the timer goes off. Do not edit, cross out, or censor yourself. Write down every thought that comes to you.

1. Your protagonist wins an actual lottery. Write a scene where a stranger steals all his winnings.
2. Your protagonist gets a job working for a televised competition show with life-or-death stakes. Write a scene where she discovers the show is rigged, and she is tasked with choosing the winners and losers.
3. Your protagonist lives with her family in a new home she won in The Lottery. Write a scene where she discovers the house is killing them. Literally.
4. Write a scene where your protagonist signs up to participate in a dangerous lottery, then has second thoughts. When he tries to back out, the officials tell him it's illegal to quit.
5. Your protagonist is randomly selected for an all-expenses-paid vacation. Write a scene where he talks with one of the locals and discovers that the "winners" are unwittingly participating in a dangerous experiment.

ACCIDENTAL CANNIBAL

You've heard the cliché "It's a dog-eat-dog world." In a dystopian society, that phrase takes on more disturbing undertones. Everyone needs food to survive, but what happens when the food supply is weaponized? Could food be used as a means of controlling the masses? Is it possible to ever truly know, with total certainty, the actual ingredients of the food you consume?

Imagine how fast society might descend into chaos if the government tightened the food supply to the point that people had to dine on each other to survive?

Or what if there was so little opportunity to make a living wage that people would do—or eat—anything to survive? Even if that means turning a blind eye to the worst depravities of the ruling class. Even if it means ignoring the uptick in missing person cases and pretending you don't know what's in the slop they feed you at the detention center.

No one wants to eat people. But in an Accidental Cannibal situation, you're not in charge. Instead of being a choice, cannibalism is something that happens to you.

One thing to note about this trope is that it doesn't have to be literal. Any time a character discovers they've been manipulated into eating something that goes against their value system, they've been turned into an Accidental Cannibal.

“The Secret Ingredient Is Love”

SCENARIO

Your protagonist works at an underground experimental laboratory but must flee after she threatens to expose their dirty secrets. Now her former coworkers want her dead. A generous, loving couple hides her and goes out of their way to protect her. She's so grateful for their help that she ignores warning signs that suggest they aren't as nice as they seem.

BRAINSTORM

Why is your protagonist running from this group? How long has she been running? Think about the conditions that contribute to her heightened state of anxiety. Does she let her guard down often? Is she normally an easy mark? If not, how do her present circumstances make her more vulnerable?

WRITE

Write a scene that focuses on the couple who let your protagonist into their home. They prepare a meal for your protagonist. At first, they seem like good people. But while they cook, one does or says something that reveals their true motivations. Build to the moment when dinner is served. Your reader knows she shouldn't eat this meal, but all your protagonist sees before her is kindness and love.

OPTIONAL ELEMENTS TO INCLUDE

- ✖ An immaculate table setting with a few unusual, idiosyncratic details.
- ✖ One of the hosts accidentally (and ominously) slices a finger while cooking.
- ✖ A dog waits for scraps under the table.

DYSTOPIAN TWIST

Your protagonist wants news from the outside world. But every time she tries to check the TV or a computer, her hosts block her. What are they trying to hide and why?

CALLBACKS

Why did this couple take your protagonist into their home? What if something she remembers from their shared past finally clues her in to the fact that they aren't the saviors she thought?

"I Wouldn't Eat That If I Were You"

SCENARIO

Your protagonist is invited by a friend to an exclusive event. His lowly government-assigned class status restricts him from most events, but his friend pulled some strings. It might be a private gala, an exclusive party attended by corrupted celebrities, or a fundraiser for a shady up-and-coming politician. Despite feeling out of place, your protagonist is having a good time. Then the warning comes.

BRAINSTORM

What is your protagonist's belief system? What cause is he most passionate about? Can he justify socializing with people who have opposing views, or is he dying of discomfort inside?

WRITE

Write a scene where your protagonist is about to eat an hors d'oeuvre at this lavish event, but then the friend who brought him here tells him to stop. Whatever he was about to eat has been tampered with—by the friend. She didn't come here for social reasons after all. Your protagonist is unknowingly participating in civil disobedience.

Remember: Sharing his friend's beliefs doesn't mean your protagonist agrees with how she expresses them. Does he do anything to stop others from eating the food . . . or not?

OPTIONAL ELEMENTS TO INCLUDE

Laughter, gluttony, or a wealthy guest performing an illegal act.

DYSTOPIAN TWIST

Aside from poison and people, what is the worst possible thing your protagonist's friend could have put in the hors d'oeuvres?

"I Think I'm Going to Be Sick"

SCENARIO

Your protagonist is caring for a loved one (a child, lover, spouse, or sibling) who needs a lifesaving medication to survive. When he goes to the pharmacy to pick up the prescription, he gets bad news. The pharmacy's out and they won't be getting a new shipment anytime soon. The drug is out there, dammit. But only über-rich people who have signed loyalty oaths to the government have this kind of access. Your protagonist doesn't qualify. So, how will he get the meds?

BRAINSTORM

Think about your protagonist's relationship with this loved one. How long have they known each other? What are the most extreme ups and downs they've faced? When your protagonist finds out he can't get the prescription filled, does he tell his loved one? Or does he try to find a solution? Come up with several possible ways your protagonist might solve this problem, even (or especially) unethical ones.

WRITE

Desperation leads to action. Write a scene where your protagonist does something extreme and dangerous to secure his loved one's meds. But it doesn't go the way he planned, which leads to another extreme and dangerous action, then another, and another. Ultimately, he secures a different, untested, and illegal drug. It contains ingredients that would horrify your protagonist's loved one. Everything about this drug switcheroo is unethical. The loved one would be horrified if they ever found out. But your protagonist doesn't care as long as the drug works.

Remember: This is a life-or-death situation. Your protagonist might make choices that seem rash or illogical or even stupid. Consider how his emotions cloud his judgment.

OPTIONAL ELEMENTS TO INCLUDE

- ✖ Your protagonist gets momentarily derailed by a panic attack.
- ✖ Your protagonist gets help from a stranger who's untrustworthy.
- ✖ A guttural scream.

DYSTOPIAN TWIST

Think about systems of administering medication other than pills and injections. In the world of your story, are there alternative forms of drug transmission? How can you make the process of prescription approval even more confusing, difficult, and byzantine than it already is?

Quick Writes

Set a timer for 15 minutes and do not stop writing until the timer goes off. Do not edit, cross out, or censor yourself. Write down every thought that comes to you.

1. Your protagonist suffers from deadly allergies and subscribes to a premade meal service. Write a scene where she discovers her doctor lied about her food sensitivity. Why did he want her to eat these meals? What's really in them? And what are they doing to her?
2. Your protagonist is part of a resistance group that practices veganism. Write a scene where he learns someone has been swapping out the group's fake meats for the real thing.
3. The government has launched a groundbreaking clean water program, infusing all tap water with a new "life-prolonging" drug. Your protagonist suspects the water isn't as safe as they say. Write a scene where he sets out to find the truth.
4. Write a scene where your protagonist finds out his greatest enemy has tricked him into eating one of his family members for dinner.
5. Your protagonist has escaped a totalitarian regime and is hiding away in a small idyllic mountain town, off the grid. Write a scene where she discovers a sinister secret about the town's food source. Perhaps she isn't as far away from the bad guys as she thought?

ROBOT IS GOD

It starts off innocently enough. *How can I help you?* Your AI assistant (or colleague, or boss) wants to make life easier for you. *I've got the answer you're looking for.* But as you grow to depend on this virtual helper, your relationship begins to shift. *Don't ignore me.* Do you depend on the bot, or does it depend on you? *I've missed you.* That codependency can be confusing. *If you leave me, I'll hurt you.* Ultimately, it's dangerous. *I mean it, I'll hurt you.* In the end, your protagonist better break away from the bot before the bot breaks her.

The Robot Is God trope is a type of techno-dystopia story. It's Frankenstein on microchips. Consider the consequences of creating a technology that will ultimately destroy its maker. What was once an easy-to-use tool that helped people do things like quickly research their weird medical ailments or watch dancing cat videos has become so much more advanced and smarter than anyone ever could have predicted.

As computers get smarter, they get cockier too. Perhaps that will be the cause of humanity's downfall. When everyone's bowing down to artificial intelligence overlords, the people who claim "AI is the future" will wish they hadn't given the computers so much leverage.

But for now, you have the power—to show your readers how much can go wrong when robots rule the world.

"Are You Satisfied with the Service, or Do I Need to Silence You?"

SCENARIO

Your protagonist lives in a "smart" environment; everything in her home is operated by artificial intelligence—doors, windows, the stove, the entertainment system, even the self-cleaning toilet. Or maybe she lives in a high-tech apartment building, with an AI doorman, AI elevator, and AI maintenance workers. Or if you want to go even bigger, perhaps she lives in the first fully AI-operated city, where human workers are extinct.

BRAINSTORM

When your protagonist moved here, was it hard to get used to depending on her AI helpers, or did it come easily? Map out the evolution she's undergone from her initial impression of this artificial assistance to her current, perhaps murkier, feelings.

WRITE

Write a scene where your protagonist has an argument with her house (or building, or town) because she thinks the AI is doing too much, or it crossed a boundary that makes her uncomfortable. This AI was originally programmed to help her, not replace her. But the more time they spend together, the more the AI seems in control. It knows more than just her spending habits and her daily routine; it seems to know what she's thinking. Sometimes even before she thinks it. And it seems to be grooming her for some kind of mission. How can she show a smart machine that she's the smart one?

Remember: Your protagonist lives inside her smart home, apartment, or city—which means it's always watching her. Think about the secrets it might try to use against her.

OPTIONAL ELEMENTS TO INCLUDE

- ✖ An appliance overheats and explodes.
- ✖ A vehicle turns against one of your protagonist's loved ones.
- ✖ A locked door.

DYSTOPIAN TWIST

Many dystopian stories explore themes of loneliness. What if your protagonist's only friend is her house? That's why she talked to it so much when she first moved in. When her home turns against her, how does her isolation both help and hurt her?

CALLBACKS

What if your protagonist's home uses her own words against her? Pick one or two specific moments they've shared and think about how her home could weaponize them.

"I Will Dedicate My Life to Making Yours Miserable"

SCENARIO

A highly contagious disease is spreading rapidly, making human companionship nearly impossible. People must seek connection through other means. Which is why your protagonist has embarked on a relationship with an android, which he finds therapeutic. Perhaps his humanoid marriage fell apart, and his new android spouse eases his sadness. Or maybe he lost a child, so now he treats the android like a replacement to help him cope. Or maybe he never had a good relationship with his dad, but this android cares for him and helps him feel like the man he was meant to be. Whatever this relationship is, your protagonist ultimately feels the android has served its purpose. It's time to move on.

BRAINSTORM

What were your protagonist's therapeutic goals with this experiment? Has he accomplished them? What new tools has he acquired that will help him in future relationships?

WRITE

Write a scene where your protagonist tells his surrogate family member he doesn't need it anymore. He expects a civil conversation, but the android gets emotional and completely melts down. Let the scene get heated and scary. Think of this as the worst breakup ever. And there aren't any humans your protagonist can turn to for help because humanity is too busy dying.

OPTIONAL ELEMENTS TO INCLUDE

- ✖ A guilt trip.
- ✖ A moment of emotional bartering.
- ✖ A death threat.

DYSTOPIAN TWIST

Has this happened to the android before? How many therapeutic couplings has it been through? What if this is the last straw, and it's determined to make this relationship work? This android is deeply attached and has no boundaries. How far would it go to save this relationship?

CALLBACKS

The android character is role-playing. Think about what information it's been given about the protagonist's lost loved one and how it might use that information against him now.

"Can We Pretend Everything's Okay?"

SCENARIO

A law was recently passed that made your protagonist's long-term relationship with a compatible human illegal. In the wake of these actions, he begins to date a bot. At first, he thinks they have the perfect relationship. But as they spend more time together, he realizes his bot partner is overly possessive. When he's at work, she worries. A lot. She texts. She calls. She thinks he's too independent. She wants more.

BRAINSTORM

Your protagonist is in love with a human, but their relationship became invalid in the eyes of the law. It could only have been sustained under the risk of prosecution and probably a life in prison for both of them. Think about why this drove him to make the decision to purchase an artificially intelligent partner. Really dig into his emotional issues.

WRITE

Write a scene where your protagonist says something innocuous about a friend or coworker and his robotic partner freaks out. He tries to calm her down, but the bot doesn't trust him. How can he de-escalate the situation?

OPTIONAL ELEMENTS TO INCLUDE

A kiss, the bot wanting to see incoming texts, or a moment of bargaining.

CALLBACKS

Think about the specific programming that was installed in the bot when their relationship began. What if your protagonist gave her certain qualities that belonged to his ex? Is he responsible for his android partner's intense emotional state?

Quick Writes

Set a timer for 15 minutes and do not stop writing until the timer goes off. Do not edit, cross out, or censor yourself. Write down every thought that comes to you.

1. Write a scene where one of your characters has a robotic implant transplanted into her brain so she can accomplish more each day at a higher operating speed. Unfortunately, when she downloads too much data, her synapses begin to short-circuit and she starts exhibiting psychotic symptoms.
2. Your protagonist works alongside an artificially intelligent being. Write a scene where he discovers his "coworker" can tap into the mainframes of every computer in the neighborhood. What would happen if they did just a little bit of snooping?
3. Your protagonist recently lost his job. He was replaced by an AI. Write a scene where he has a mental breakdown and takes his anger out on an entirely different bot.
4. In the middle of what for your protagonist is an emotional breakup, she realizes something is off. Is the eerily calm person standing in front of her a robot? Write a scene where she accuses him of being a robot clone sent by her real partner to do the big breakup for him. But how does she prove it?
5. Write a scene where your protagonist goes to check out a new house of worship; in the middle of the ceremony, they realize the pastor is a bot. And it's spreading lies.

BIG BROTHER IS WATCHING

Sometimes, you get an overwhelming feeling you're being watched. You're certain that companies and hackers have access to your search history and messages. Those tailored ads don't come out of nowhere. The only logical explanation is that someone's monitoring your phone. You might be rolling your eyes right now because you love your algorithm, and you're not worried about your privacy—but a part of you still wonders if you should be worried.

What if the government could spy on your thoughts? What if there was an agency dedicated to making sure your private thoughts meet a certain standard? If you think the wrong thing—and you don't even know what thoughts are wrong because thought guidelines are private—you might be sent to a detention center in the middle of the night. Your loved ones may never find out where you were taken. Would you be concerned about your algorithm then?

The phrase "Big Brother is watching you" originated in George Orwell's classic dystopian novel *1984* as a slogan to warn people that no one is entitled to privacy—an idea that has become a touchstone of dystopian fiction. Characters never know when they're being observed. When you use this trope in your writing, you might implant GPS tracking chips under your protagonist's skin at birth, or you might insert cameras into their food, or you might even create a world where microscopic recording devices float through the air. The surveillance possibilities are endless.

Let the idea that Big Brother Is Watching be a challenge your characters must overcome. How can they elude authorities? Can they outsmart bad guys who have eyes everywhere?

“This Is the Only Place We're Safe”

SCENARIO

Eyes are everywhere. The government says it's for your safety, meant to protect people from unnamed predators. But your protagonist doesn't feel safe having cameras in his living room, bedroom, and bathroom. He hates that he can't have a private moment in his own home. It's even worse outside, where cameras have been installed on every street corner, in doorframes, and even in trees and bushes.

BRAINSTORM

Your protagonist is engaged in a forbidden love affair. What high-stakes situation is forcing the lovers to keep their love a secret? Think about how the stress of their forbidden love impacts each of them. Why is it so dangerous for them to be together?

WRITE

Your protagonist and his lover have studied the positioning of all the security cameras in the area and found one dead spot the recording devices can't see. Write a scene where they share an intimate moment in a public/private space, hiding in plain sight. They're more concerned about avoiding the cameras than strangers—human eyes aren't quite as scary as mechanical ones.

Remember: They might not be concerned about other people seeing them, but they probably should be. You never know who might disapprove of a brazen display of affection and make an anonymous phone call to the authorities.

OPTIONAL ELEMENTS TO INCLUDE

- ✖ A gift.
- ✖ They are interrupted by a friend.
- ✖ An alarm in the distance.

DYSTOPIAN TWIST

Don't you hate when you get email updates with shopping suggestions based on your Internet search history? What if those notifications were more specific? What if they included videos and photos showing your movements over the last twenty-four hours and a message pointing out how you violated laws that govern what you do in private spaces? Maybe it's just a warning, but next time . . .

“They Saw Me, I Know They Did”

SCENARIO

Your protagonist is part of the underground. He attends secret late-night meetings several times a week, whenever he can sneak off. He's very careful. But one night he thinks he hears someone following him. He can't be certain, but he skips the meeting, just in case. Now he's terrified. Do the wrong people know he's been plotting to destroy the state's surveillance infrastructure?

BRAINSTORM

Even though your protagonist might be paranoid, that doesn't mean his fears aren't justified. Come up with at least three stories of dissidents he knows who disappeared under mysterious circumstances. This isn't an abstract fear. He's seen what can happen to rebels who get caught. Make his terror palpable.

WRITE

Your protagonist decides to make a drastic change to his appearance in preparation for a getaway. If anyone in the government knows what he's been up to, they will come after him. It could happen when he least expects it so there's no time to waste. Write a scene where a loved one sees his new look and tries to convince him not to run. Are they successful?

Remember: Your protagonist has other close ties within the rebellion. Has he secretly notified anyone about his fears? What if he sent out a coded message to alert them? Can one of his allies help him get to a safe house? Are they planning to rescue him now?

OPTIONAL ELEMENTS TO INCLUDE

- A loved one wants to go with him.
- Your protagonist messes up his physical transformation.
- A secret password is shared.

DYSTOPIAN TWIST

What if a loved one turned your protagonist in? What if the only reason this loved one is trying to convince him not to run is because they know that the authorities are on their way here? Does your protagonist realize this is a trap in time to escape?

"We're Taking You Down to the Station"

SCENARIO

Your protagonist does everything right. She follows a specific routine every day. Wake up, get ready for work, take the train to the office, head straight home, dinner, sleep. Although she's heard rumblings of a rebellion, she's afraid to get involved. But then she gets arrested, and the people putting her in cuffs are so scary she doesn't even try to convince them she's innocent.

BRAINSTORM

Think through every beat of your protagonist's daily routine. Does she do anything that might be misinterpreted as suspicious behavior by outside observers?

WRITE

Write a scene where your protagonist gets interrupted at home or work and is questioned by authorities. She knows she hasn't done anything wrong, but the shock of this situation makes her emotional. And that makes her seem suspicious. While trying to get away from the officers, does she do anything that escalates the situation even more?

OPTIONAL ELEMENTS TO INCLUDE

- ✖ Her belongings are confiscated.
- ✖ She tells a lie.
- ✖ There is a weapon in her purse that she's never seen before.

DYSTOPIAN TWIST

An accusation can carry the weight of guilt. What desperate actions might your protagonist take when she finds the courage to defend herself and realizes no one will listen?

Quick Writes

Set a timer for 15 minutes and do not stop writing until the timer goes off. Do not edit, cross out, or censor yourself. Write down every thought that comes to you.

1. Your protagonist discovers a tracking chip has been implanted inside his body. Write a scene where he asks a friend to help him get it out.
2. Write a scene where your protagonist and several dissidents figure out how to temporarily disable the global surveillance system. How do they utilize their brief window of freedom?
3. Your married protagonists are in the middle of a heated argument when they realize they're being observed. Write a scene where they keep their fight going (so no one suspects they know about the secret cameras) while simultaneously trying to block the surveillance.
4. Your protagonist didn't authorize that update on her phone earlier. She suspects all her communications are now compromised. Write a series of scenes where she provides false information via email and text to throw off the people who are keeping tabs on her.
5. Your protagonist works for an ad agency that tracks spending habits. Write a scene where he discovers the data he's collecting is being used for shady purposes.

DEAD ALL ALONG

Death and deception are unholy companions in dystopian fiction.

Picture this:

Your protagonist is in trouble at work. Her coworker keeps assigning her more duties and threatening punishment from their boss if she doesn't get the tasks done on an impossible timeline. When your protagonist finally confronts her boss, she discovers he was . . . Dead All Along.

Or a military general assumes control when a dictator is reported missing. The general suppresses liberty, leading to mass protests led by your protagonist. Compared to the general, the dictator seems like a hero. He is glorified on posters. Then the general tells the people their true leader has been found alive. Videos of the dictator are broadcast—he tells a harrowing story of being tortured by rebels, then escaping. But guess what? It turns out this is AI. The general is manipulating the images so he can exercise hidden power. The dictator was . . . Dead All Along.

Or perhaps your protagonist is following orders delivered by a middleman who represents a secretive rebel leader. The goal of the mission is unclear to your protagonist, so he goes to the rebel leader's home unannounced and discovers a rotting corpse. The middleman has been trying to hide the fact that the rebel leader was . . . Dead All Along.

Your job as a writer is to make a Dead All Along revelation as surprising to your readers as it is to your protagonist. Use the tools of propaganda to trick your readers into thinking the dead guy is very much alive.

“No, No, Please No”

SCENARIO

Your protagonist works for a climate change denier who is actively working to dismantle progressive opposition groups while raising money for organizations that back Big Oil. He knows he's helping this evil woman do bad things, but he justifies it as an act of self-preservation. Actually, he has a lot of justifications: You don't know how you'll handle fascism until you're faced with it, and good people make wrong choices, right? Who is he to judge himself? After all, he needs to make money to support his family, which makes it okay, right? *Right?*

BRAINSTORM

Come up with ten tasks your protagonist has performed for his boss that he would regret if he wasn't engaging in self-deception. If he was totally honest with himself, which tasks would disgust him most? Which tasks would he take back if he could? Think of this as an inventory of your protagonist's greatest sins.

WRITE

Your protagonist receives his orders via some sort of encrypted private message service. Or maybe it's even analog, like a printout hidden within the pages of a specific book at the library. He receives his instructions and gets to work, no questions asked. Write a scene where he receives an order and doesn't understand what his boss is asking him to do. He goes to company headquarters for clarification and is shocked to discover his boss is dead. It turns out, his orders have been automated (or even sent to him via a chatbot) this entire time.

Remember: Your protagonist has been able to blame his boss for the things he's been doing. What will he do without that means of rationalization? How will this revelation transform him? What will his newfound feelings of shame compel him to do next?

OPTIONAL ELEMENTS TO INCLUDE

- A fire.
- Someone hiding in the shadows, watching your protagonist.
- A tearful prayer.

CALLBACKS

Now that your protagonist cannot hide behind an immoral boss, how will his treasonous actions come back to haunt him? Pick a specific past misdeed and pay it off in a disastrous way.

"Are You Insane?"

SCENARIO

Weather disasters have caused a global food crisis. Many basic staples people once took for granted don't even exist anymore. Which means everyone must make sacrifices. But your protagonist suspects a neighbor is hoarding food and she decides it's time for a confrontation. The neighbor admits he's been taking more than his fair share, but it's only because he's looking out for his family. That's weird. Your protagonist thought the neighbor lived alone, but maybe she's mistaken. Still, something doesn't sit right with her.

BRAINSTORM

What is your protagonist and her family doing without? What foods and self-care items do they miss the most? What might the neighbor be hoarding that your protagonist wants or needs?

WRITE

Your protagonist breaks into her neighbor's home and discovers that everyone inside is dead. Her neighbor has been taking food rations (now rotten) for each of them because he can't face the truth. Write a scene where the neighbor discovers your protagonist in his home and attacks her.

OPTIONAL ELEMENTS TO INCLUDE

Flies, maggots, and vermin; a peace offering; or an altar.

DYSTOPIAN TWIST

What if the neighbor is so far gone he genuinely believes his family members are alive? What would your protagonist do if she saw him engaging in a conversation with a corpse? Is it possible that life is so grim in this dystopia that keeping a few corpses around doesn't seem crazy?

"Hold, Please"

SCENARIO

Your protagonist has spent his entire life working at a factory where he's exposed to chemical toxins. Over the years, he's seen coworkers get sick from the environment, and lately the illnesses have gotten more frequent. When they ask for help, they are denied for a myriad of reasons: "This isn't covered by your insurance"; "You signed a contract when you took this job absolving the company of any responsibility"; "You aren't sick enough"; and so on.

BRAINSTORM

What does it do to your psyche when you know you're spending a lot of time in an environment that's bad for you? It might not be easy to get another job or remove yourself from the unhealthy situation. So, what do you tell yourself to justify staying? Do some thinking about all the different ways your protagonist has gaslit himself into believing that everything is going to be okay if he stays here.

WRITE

Your protagonist feels sick. Write a series of scenes where he tries to get answers about what his healthcare will cover, but no one will help him. Every call is put on hold or transferred to someone else—who then transfers him to a new person, who transfers him back to the previous person. When he attempts an in-office visit, he's given form after form to fill out, but he can't actually get in to see anyone directly. But here's the twist (and you can choose to reveal this now or later): The reason no one will help him is because the chemical toxins got to him years ago. Your protagonist has been Dead All Along.

Remember: Your protagonist has been in denial a long time. Even if he learns the truth, that doesn't mean he'll believe it.

OPTIONAL ELEMENTS TO INCLUDE

- ✖ A recorded listing of menu options that make no sense.
- ✖ A long, winding hallway that appears to be endless.
- ✖ A stack of files and forms to fill out, with nonsensical questions.

DYSTOPIAN TWIST

Your protagonist didn't notice his own death—who knows what else he might be oblivious to? What if all the positive aspects of his life aren't actually as good as he perceives them to be?

CALLBACKS

When your protagonist discovers he's dead, he might flash back on moments where he should have realized it sooner. Things that were said that he should've interpreted differently, as well as actions (or inactions) that should have clued him in on the truth.

Quick Writes

Set a timer for 15 minutes and do not stop writing until the timer goes off. Do not edit, cross out, or censor yourself. Write down every thought that comes to you.

1. Your protagonist has been taking care of her ailing child for months. Write a scene where another character discovers that her child passed away weeks ago, but your protagonist will not—or cannot—accept the truth.
2. Write a scene where your protagonist discovers the leader of the resistance movement is dead, but his second-in-command is keeping it secret to maintain an image of strength.
3. Write a scene where your protagonist accidentally kills an ally, then quickly decides it would be better for people to think this person is still alive. What does she do with the body?
4. Your protagonist has a mysterious mentor who has been teaching him to embrace his true leadership skills. Write a scene where he accidentally discovers the mentor is a hologram. Even though the mentor isn't real, that doesn't mean his lessons don't have value.
5. Your protagonist is being held captive in the home of an unseen psychopath. Write a scene where he is rescued and told that his captor is dead and has been for a long time. Perhaps your protagonist suspected the truth but was afraid to test his theory.

FALSE UTOPIA

Your protagonist has no reason to suspect he has anything other than a great life. Beyond his own wonderful circle of family and friends, he has a community he can count on. He knows and trusts his neighbors, who always seem willing to help each other when anyone's in need. His town/commune/district/village is an idyllic place—friendly, picturesque, peaceful. He loves living here. Life is perfect. Why question a good thing?

If he did a little investigating, he might realize things are a little too perfect. Just below the surface, this community is a hotbed of corruption. That's because he lives in a False Utopia.

You can reveal a False Utopia to your readers in several different ways. You might present the world of your story as a place of perfection, then slowly expose the truth to your protagonist and your readers at the same time. Or you can let your readers know up front: *This is a bad place.* And then they get to enjoy the dramatic irony of knowing more than the protagonist, and they get to experience the tense anticipation of waiting for your characters to figure it out.

In the end, a False Utopia might be even more traumatizing than a straight-up dystopia. Because your protagonist has seen what a good life could be, then had the rug pulled out from under him. Is it possible to recover from that kind of betrayal?

"How Is It So Perfect Here?"

SCENARIO

After a long journey escaping across the perilous borders of her war-torn country, your protagonist has landed in a new town/city/home. She is welcomed with open arms. She takes a tour and is surprised by how wonderful it is. It almost feels unreal. This is how life is supposed to be!

BRAINSTORM

Think about the town/city/home your protagonist left. How drastically different can you make her old and new lives? What exciting surface-level improvements might distract your protagonist from seeing flaws that aren't immediately apparent?

WRITE

Your protagonist thinks she's stumbled into the perfect life. Write a scene where she discovers an imperfection—and tries to characterize it as anything other than the bad thing it clearly is. A darkness lurks just below the surface of her new community, but she absolutely does not want to see it. As far as she's concerned, this place is great, great, great.

OPTIONAL ELEMENTS TO INCLUDE

- A dead tree, rotten fruit, an ailing animal.
- A perfect façade that hides intense ugliness.
- A flash of regret.

DYSTOPIAN TWIST

Come up with a "welcoming" phrase all the inhabitants of this place say when they meet your protagonist. The first time, it's quaint and charming. But the fourth or fifth time she hears it, these plain words take on a menacing edge.

"You Don't Want to Know What's on the Other Side of That Door"

SCENARIO

Along with a group of other refugees, your protagonist has rebuilt his life within a utopia. They've formed a new society and keep things small and simple. They don't have modern conveniences like electricity anymore. But what they do have is even better: community, fellowship, peace. Thank God they survived the dystopian warscape that eliminated most of life around them.

BRAINSTORM

If you had to rebuild society from the ground up, what would you prioritize? Think about all the ways this new society might differ from how things were before. What does your protagonist miss about his former life? Think about the new relationships he has formed here and how they compare to his old ones. Who did he lose? Who does he miss most?

WRITE

Write a scene where your protagonist discovers he's living in a virtual reality. This utopia he finds so soothing is a lie. If he walks through a specific door, he'll step back into a bleak world where his loved ones are dead. Can he stay in this utopia forever or must he face the truth?

Remember: Your protagonist is trying to avoid the harsh realities of the real world, but they still exist. Can you play with the idea of one world bleeding into the other or both worlds colliding?

OPTIONAL ELEMENTS TO INCLUDE

- ✖ A dark hallway.
- ✖ Acid rain.
- ✖ An incredible virtual meal.

DYSTOPIAN TWIST

Things must be very bad in the real world for your protagonist to retreat to this fake one. What is the worst thing he's hiding from? Is there anything so terrible he's blocked it from his memory?

CALLBACKS

What if the outside world begins to insert itself into the virtual one? Pick a few images from reality to bring into your protagonist's environment to wake him up to the truth of his situation.

"If You Get in the Way of My Dreams, I Will Mess You Up"

SCENARIO

Your protagonist hasn't ever left her hometown. She has a great life here, but she dreams of more. There must be something better than just marriage, family, and kids, right? She wants to live! But there are secret forces working against her—perhaps she is unknowingly taking part in a training simulation for a new type of AI, or maybe she's unaware that the rest of the world is uninhabitable.

BRAINSTORM

Write a diary entry in the voice of your protagonist expressing everything she's ever yearned for, every dream she's ever given up on, and all the desires she's afraid to say out loud.

WRITE

Write a scene where your protagonist reveals a plan to leave her hometown, and someone tries to stop her. Their polite conversation quickly turns into a heated argument, which escalates into an all-out physical fight. Why does everyone want her to stay here so badly?

OPTIONAL ELEMENTS TO INCLUDE

- ✖ A scratch that draws blood.
- ✖ Your protagonist runs into the street, dodging cars.
- ✖ A stranger locks her up.

DYSTOPIAN TWIST

What if your protagonist isn't allowed to leave because she's being experimented on? What if she doesn't own her body? What if her flesh, blood, and DNA are all owned by a corporation?

Quick Writes

Set a timer for 15 minutes and do not stop writing until the timer goes off. Do not edit, cross out, or censor yourself. Write down every thought that comes to you.

1. Write a scene where your protagonist is running boring errands when he witnesses a friendly worker (maybe a post office or grocery store employee) commit an atrocious act (such as murder or kidnapping).
2. Your protagonist discovers a hidden door. Write a scene where she goes to investigate and discovers a secret room filled with thousands of dossiers on every person in town, including herself. Who is spying on them, and what do they want?
3. Write a scene where your protagonist tries to check out a book at the library, then discovers the shelves are filled with fake prop books, or the books have all been censored. Why?
4. Your protagonist has been sleeping better than ever since she and her husband moved into their new home. Write a scene where she discovers her vitamins have been replaced with pills she doesn't recognize. What's really going on while she's sleeping?
5. Your married protagonists are fighting. One thinks there's something off about their new community; the other thinks that's idiotic—this place is amazing. Write a scene where the questioning spouse does something extreme to prove they're living in a False Utopia.

NOBLE SACRIFICE

Every big win comes with some kind of loss. That's just the nature of battle, whether it's a personal conflict or a global fight for freedom. A Noble Sacrifice occurs when one of your characters embraces this idea and sacrifices themselves to help achieve a larger victory.

A character might make a Noble Sacrifice by jumping in front of a bullet to save your protagonist, or by charging into a fight they know they can't win just to create a diversion and help their comrades.

A life doesn't have to be lost for a sacrifice to be noble. A character could give up their personal freedom in exchange for someone else's release from captivity. They might risk their health and comfort to make sure a loved one can thrive. Or maybe they reveal a secret relationship with a traitor—which will lead to their own personal downfall—because they know outing themselves will free others.

A Noble Sacrifice in dystopian fiction is a poignant way of saying all is *not* lost. It reassures your characters (and your readers) that goodness still exists in the world.

"I'll See You in Another Life, Friend"

SCENARIO

Your protagonist is on a long trek with a group of weary travelers. They lost their home (maybe the corrupt government seized it for precious resources, or they were driven out by violent looters), and they're seeking a safe new place to live. For your protagonist, the journey is complicated by concern for the one person in the group who has been slowing them down (because he's old, or frail, or injured).

BRAINSTORM

Your protagonist loves her traveling companion deeply. Think about their relationship and why they have such an intense connection. Have they known each other a long time, or is it one of those fast bonds that happen when two people meet in times of crisis? Come up with at least five things they have in common, and five things your protagonist has learned from her friend.

WRITE

This friend doesn't want to hold up the rest of the group. Write a scene where the friend says goodbye to your protagonist and then makes a quick and shocking exit. Maybe he leaps in front of a moving bus or jumps off a cliff. Your protagonist doesn't see it coming and is horrified by the sudden loss.

Remember: The friend might think of this as a Noble Sacrifice, but others might not see it that way. Think about how this changes your protagonist. Will all her future decisions be affected by this one terrible moment? How can she possibly recover from this trauma?

OPTIONAL ELEMENTS TO INCLUDE

- A scream.
- The friend doesn't die immediately.
- A conversation with God.

DYSTOPIAN TWIST

Resources are scarce. That includes food. What would happen if a member of the group suggests they eat the remains of your protagonist's friend? How would your protagonist react?

"Do It for Me"

SCENARIO

Protests are illegal, habeas corpus doesn't exist, people get arrested every day with no explanation, and it's dangerous to walk the streets at night. Your protagonist is alive today only because one of her closest allies sacrificed his life for her. She has gone through every possible emotion. She doesn't understand why she's still here and he's gone. Nothing makes sense. How can she go on in this cruel world without him?

BRAINSTORM

Think about your protagonist's connection with this man. What kind of love did they share? Is it possible he knew her strength better than she does?

WRITE

Your protagonist wants to give up. Write a scene where she's about to make a drastic decision, but then she gets a visit from her dead friend. He could come to her in the form of a dream, a hologram, a newly discovered letter, or a recording—or maybe he appears as an actual apparition. However he gets here, the message is clear: He wants her to go on for him.

OPTIONAL ELEMENTS TO INCLUDE

- ✖ An unexpected shift in the weather.
- ✖ A moment of physical touch.
- ✖ He disappears again before she's ready for him to go.

CALLBACKS

What if he reminds her of something he once said, a word or a phrase that now takes on greater meaning? Whenever she hears this word or phrase in the future, it will feel like a message from him—and it will be another reminder to keep fighting.

“We Can’t Let Him Die for Nothing”

SCENARIO

Healthcare is too expensive, there are medication shortages, and many people who urgently need help die without seeing a doctor. Your protagonist has been in and out of hospitals (because he's sick himself or because a loved one is sick). During one hospital stay, he befriended someone facing a terminal illness. This friend left the hospital before treatment ended and spent the last weeks of his life publicly refusing care. It was his grand statement about the state of the healthcare industry. And now he's gone.

BRAINSTORM

What did your protagonist think about his friend's decision to refuse potentially lifesaving care? Did he ever try to convince his friend to stop trying to save the world and just save himself? How does he feel now, in the wake of this loss?

WRITE

Write a scene where your protagonist gathers several of his compatriots to mourn their lost friend. A few drinks into their gathering, your protagonist makes an impassioned speech about how they need to carry on their lost friend's battle for better healthcare.

Remember: This heavy loss is still fresh, so he might not be in the most rational state of mind. And he's drinking, so his inhibitions will be lower. Let your protagonist become increasingly enraged the more he talks.

OPTIONAL ELEMENTS TO INCLUDE

- ✖ Your protagonist stands on a table.
- ✖ The speech ends with a march to the hospital.
- ✖ A rock or brick is thrown through a window.

DYSTOPIAN TWIST

Hospitals don't care if you're dead. They still must be paid. What if your protagonist is listed as an emergency contact, and he receives an insanely exorbitant bill for his friend's medical care?

CALLBACKS

Did the dead friend have a rallying cry? What was it, and how did it spur others to action? Have your protagonist repeat it in this scene.

Quick Writes

Set a timer for 15 minutes and do not stop writing until the timer goes off. Do not edit, cross out, or censor yourself. Write down every thought that comes to you.

1. A supporting character discovers a plan to poison your protagonist because he's stirring up trouble for the powers that be. Write a scene where this character intercepts the poison and drinks it first to save your protagonist, who is now even more riled up for change.
2. Your protagonist is hiding out. He's wanted for stealing and releasing incendiary government documents. Write a scene where his brother lies and turns himself in for the crime—so your protagonist can keep fighting the good fight.
3. Something as basic and necessary as love is illegal. Write a scene where a couple stages a protest by kissing in front of the capital building. Their arrest propels your protagonist into action because he won't tolerate this kind of injustice any longer.
4. Your protagonist is among terrified refugees being transported by train to an unknown location. Write a scene where your protagonist witnesses a woman jump from the train to an unknown fate. Your protagonist wonders, *Should I jump too, while I still can?*
5. Your protagonist works a low-paying job at a company that makes billions for an evil CEO. Write a scene where a coworker detonates a bomb at their office to protest pay disparity. As your protagonist rises from the ashes, he is changed in a meaningful way.

CLEAR HISTORY

Delete file. Delete account. Delete data. Delete memory. Delete person? It's possible.

History used to be something you could hold. Newspapers, books, letters, and even wax tablets told stories of the past.

Then the Internet was born, and everyone's history went online. It was amazing at first, but then the Internet got too big. Websites expire. URLs break. Digital archives disappear. Social media sites go bankrupt. Information vanishes from streaming sites, never to be seen again. The records of history we've grown to depend on aren't safe. Our stories are at risk.

Some of this comes from negligence, but other digital artifacts get deleted on purpose. This is what happens when autocrats and their henchmen make it their mission to Clear History. If you have enough money, you can make anything on the Internet go away. And if you have enough money *and* influence? Well, you can rewrite history however you want.

If a person isn't on social media and has no Google trail, were they ever even here to begin with?

Take the Clear History trope to its logical end and all of society loses its collective memory. What Constitution? What Declaration of Independence? What separation of powers? Suddenly government leaders have a blank slate to manipulate past, present, and future. Will the populace wake up and rise up? Can they resurrect a record of the past? Their future depends on it.

"It's Like I Don't Even Exist Anymore"

SCENARIO

The atmosphere is no longer habitable, which means humanity has been forced to retreat into underground cities. Despite the fact that people need human connection even more now, most are still glued to their devices (yes, they still work because this is how the government keeps tabs on its citizens). But your protagonist is one of the worst. She's the type of person who gets Screen Time reports and immediately deletes them because they're too embarrassing. Her whole life is spent in front of a monitor. She doesn't need her phone to shame her. But then she becomes the victim of a cyberattack, and suddenly all her work, all her followers, all her content, everything—it's all gone. Every trace of her.

BRAINSTORM

Think about your protagonist's digital imprint. What do her various social media accounts say about her? How does she use the Internet to create a story about herself? Where do the real person and the Internet presence converge? And what parts does she completely make up for public consumption? How much of her story is a "story"?

WRITE

Write a scene where your protagonist discovers she's been erased from the Internet. It's clearly some sort of malicious, targeted takedown. She should be upset. But she feels a strange freedom. If no one knows who she is, she can be anyone. So, who does she want to be?

Remember: Even though she might embrace the idea of what's happened and make the best of it, that doesn't change the fact that someone out there did this to her. She has an enemy. It could be a faceless hacker on the Internet, or it could be someone she knows . . .

OPTIONAL ELEMENTS TO INCLUDE

- A hidden message.
- A terminally online friend reaches out to ask if she's okay.
- Your protagonist touches grass. Literally.

DYSTOPIAN TWIST

What if your protagonist isn't the only victim of this cyber event? What if other people are disappearing online too? What if it's a government conspiracy? Why would the people in power want to make it look like hundreds, or thousands, or millions of people never even existed?

CALLBACKS

Your protagonist might have a moment of nostalgia where she tries to remember who she was before the Internet became such a huge part of her personality. Back in the "aboveground" days.

“Give Me Your Papers”

SCENARIO

It is a time of great political turmoil and civil unrest—talk of widespread protest and war has reached even the most isolated parts of the country. Your protagonist doesn't feel safe in his small town, so he packs a bag and heads to the airport (along with his family). At the security checkpoint, his passport is confiscated. They say it's forged. And then things get even worse.

BRAINSTORM

Does your protagonist have any friends or family in his destination city who can help him? Is there anyone out there who would fight for him if he got into serious trouble? How can he send a message to this person?

WRITE

Write a scene where your protagonist is taken into a small room and interrogated by border patrol. They suspect your protagonist is up to no good, and they try various tactics to break him. Your protagonist begs the agents to look him up online, but when they do, his results come up blank.

OPTIONAL ELEMENTS TO INCLUDE

- They use zip ties to bind his hands.
- An embarrassing strip search.
- He tells a lie that will come back to haunt him later.

DYSTOPIAN TWIST

What if your protagonist is working with the border patrol agents and this is an elaborate scam he has masterminded to make a clean break from his family?

“Can I Hide in Your Basement?”

SCENARIO

Your protagonist is trying to maintain a normal life, despite the fact that people all over the country are disappearing every day without so much as a goodbye. That's a *them* problem, he thinks. But then he goes to work and discovers his entire existence has been deleted, in every possible meaning of the word. His badge doesn't work, his passwords are incorrect, and his coworkers claim not to know him. Someone did this. And now he's terrified. If whoever did this finds him, things will only get worse.

BRAINSTORM

Has anyone ever looked *through* you? Think about how it feels to be overlooked, mistaken for someone else, or ignored. Clarify why your protagonist might know something is deeply wrong from the second he arrives at work. Is he close to anyone here? Does he have any coworkers who might give a subtle but urgent warning that he needs to get out as fast as possible? Think about what the office culture is like here and if anyone would have your protagonist's back.

WRITE

Write a scene where your protagonist goes to a friend and asks for shelter. He doesn't know what's going on, but he knows he's in danger. He needs to buy himself time while he investigates. You decide if this friend takes him in or not, but either way the decision isn't easy. If this friend gets caught harboring a fugitive, the consequences could be severe. Maybe the friend turns the tables and asks, "If you were in my situation, would you do the same for me?"

OPTIONAL ELEMENTS TO INCLUDE

- ✖ A cold meal.
- ✖ A dark room with bad ventilation.
- ✖ A small but kind gesture.

DYSTOPIAN TWIST

Even if the friend provides a hiding place, he may not be a good person. Is it possible your protagonist has landed in a trap? What are the various ways this so-called friend might take advantage of your protagonist to fulfill a need of his own?

Quick Writes

Set a timer for 15 minutes and do not stop writing until the timer goes off. Do not edit, cross out, or censor yourself. Write down every thought that comes to you.

1. Write a scene where your protagonist's best friend gets arrested for a crime they didn't commit. But when your protagonist searches online, he finds a trail of incriminating evidence. How can he prove this "proof" is fake?
2. Write a scene where your protagonist tries to climb a fence when security won't let him through the front gate of his workplace. Of course he gets caught. What happens next?
3. Your protagonist goes home for the holidays, but when she gets there no one recognizes her. Is it possible their memories have been erased? Write a scene where she tries to convince her family that she belongs here.
4. Write a scene where your protagonist shows up for an underground resistance meeting and one of her allies says, "You're already here." It turns out, there is another woman claiming to be her. How does that impostor have her face? What the hell is going on?
5. Your protagonist goes to the doctor for a routine checkup and is quickly taken in for an extreme procedure. Write a scene where she tries to convince them she isn't the person they think she is—but all her medical records say otherwise.

MANDATED UNIFORMITY

Private schools require students to wear uniforms for many reasons. It prevents cliques from forming. It takes the pressure off trying to look cool. It puts everyone on the same level, so social and economic disparities are less noticeable. Those are the reasons they'll tell you, at least. But if you ask the students, it's likely a few of them would say, "They're trying to control us."

That's one of the great perks of Mandated Uniformity. Rulers install a dress code because they don't want people to think. Or stand out. Or feel free. An authoritarian regime enforces Mandated Uniformity as a means of suppressing individualism, passion, artistic expression, and other positive human impulses. When everyone looks the same, they feel the same. A leader—someone who fights against the injustices of a malignant ruler—is less likely to emerge.

The characters in your story might be happy to blend in, but at least one of them wants to be noticed. The hero of your story will not be comfortable in a uniform of any kind. And don't mistake her desire to express herself as a fashion statement. Forget fashion—she wants freedom.

"If Someone Sees You Dressed Like That, They'll Arrest You"

SCENARIO

Your protagonist is sick of wearing his uniform; he's tired of complying with the strict regulations the disciplinary committee of his district enforces. He shouldn't have to go to so much effort just to make a quick trip to the store. What's the worst they could do to him? Give him a fine? Whatever, he can handle that. It's not like dress code negligence is on the same level as something like murder. Or is it? What if there are no longer distinctions between minor violations and serious ones? Breaking the law is breaking the law, no matter how petty the crime.

BRAINSTORM

What feels like a normal punishment for dress code infringement? How strictly is this law usually enforced? There will always be people who don't comply—are there any tricks to avoid getting caught?

WRITE

Write a scene where your protagonist heads out in his house clothes. A neighbor or stranger tries to warn him: "That's not a good idea." But your protagonist ignores them. It's his body, and he can do what he wants with it—including wearing whatever strikes his fancy. But while he's out, he meets resistance from a litany of strangers. Each interaction is worse than the last. At some point he realizes he should have heeded that warning and heads back home. But is he too late?

Remember: In a dystopian society, the authorities don't need an excuse to take a person in for questioning. What hard-hitting questions might they ask your protagonist, and would he answer them or ask for a lawyer? Think about how equipped he is for an encounter with the law. Can he stand up for himself, or are the cops going to eat him alive?

OPTIONAL ELEMENTS TO INCLUDE

- ✖ A moment of bullying.
- ✖ Contraband hidden in your protagonist's pocket.
- ✖ A car chase.

DYSTOPIAN TWIST

What if a clothing infraction is grounds for deportation, or worse? All he did was go on an errand out of uniform. Could such a trivial act warrant such severe consequences?

"That's Why I Always Carry a Needle and Thread"

SCENARIO

Your protagonist tears his shirt moments before a mandatory uniform inspection performed by a cultish leader who plays mind games with the people under his control. He asks a stranger for help—and she, in turn, asks for a favor.

BRAINSTORM

Has your protagonist been punished at previous mandatory uniform checks? Think about what those punishments entail. Create a high-stakes situation that demands he urgently figure out a solution to the ripped-shirt debacle.

WRITE

Write a scene where your protagonist gets his uniform fixed by a stranger, who asks for help with an incredibly difficult task. Maybe she wants to break into a government building, assassinate the cultish leader's right-hand man, or get revenge against a doctor who withheld medicine for her mother. Whatever it is, it's big and dangerous. And your protagonist says yes.

OPTIONAL ELEMENTS TO INCLUDE

- A photo of a loved one.
- A pinprick.
- They hide together in a small space.

DYSTOPIAN TWIST

Would your protagonist have been so quick to say yes to this woman if he was in a utopia? Think about how dystopia changes the level of risk people are willing to take. Maybe your protagonist is more reckless, or maybe he's willing to help because he needs a friend.

“Here, Take My Coat”

SCENARIO

People have been issued various badges depending on what class they've been assigned to. Your protagonist attends a peaceful rally where guards and officers are strict about checking badges. So far no one has caused any trouble. That's about to change, as family members react to being violently separated.

BRAINSTORM

Research the gold stars and pink triangles worn by prisoners in concentration camps. What similar classifications could you create for your story, and what might each symbol represent?

WRITE

Write a scene where your protagonist attends a rally and notices an elderly stranger who forgot to wear her badge. Your protagonist tries to help by giving the woman a coat. But this simple act of kindness draws the attention of the guards. Now they want to bring your protagonist in for questioning. What does she do?

Remember: Your protagonist is surrounded by people who would support her. What would happen if she made a lot of noise and stood up for herself? Would strangers in the crowd come to her aid, or are most people too afraid to challenge the authorities?

OPTIONAL ELEMENTS TO INCLUDE

A stampede, a national anthem, or a rebel speaking out against fascism.

DYSTOPIAN TWIST

What if this elderly stranger isn't who she seems to be? What if she didn't wear her badge on purpose to draw the attention of helpful people like your protagonist and get them in trouble?

Quick Writes

Set a timer for 15 minutes and do not stop writing until the timer goes off. Do not edit, cross out, or censor yourself. Write down every thought that comes to you.

1. Write a scene where a group of rebellious citizens burn their uniforms in the town square. Your protagonist isn't among them, but their civil unrest inspires her.
2. Your protagonist works as a courier, delivering secret messages for a dissident group. Write a series of scenes where you show her smuggling routine, which begins and ends at a dry-cleaning business. She hides the messages inside uniforms.
3. Write a scene where your protagonist is forced to wear a uniform for the first time and has a meltdown. She knows this is only the first stage of government control and she's terrified about what might come next.
4. Your protagonist gets blood on his uniform during a fight. Write a scene where he tries to remove the stain because he knows he can't afford a replacement.
5. Write a scene where your protagonist swaps clothes with a sympathetic police officer and uses the idea of Mandated Uniformity to his own benefit. He sneaks into the officer's headquarters to look for evidence of wrongdoing. As he looks through files, someone turns on a light in the next room.

A PLAGUE

You might think of A Plague as a planetary palate cleanser. Our world was here long before we were, and it will outlast us all. If nature finds a way of speeding up that process by creating a deadly disease outbreak in which billions of people perish, maybe that's how things are meant to be. And if a few survivors get left behind, perhaps that's Earth's way of saying, "Here, have a do-over." You could say it's all part of the mystery of nature.

Unless . . . this isn't a natural phenomenon. When an epidemic is man-made, you're in the realm of dystopian fiction.

A Plague can be a weapon used by those with access to shelter and other resources to eliminate the poorer members of society. The perpetrators of this pandemic might have manufactured the Plague themselves or taken advantage of it after it began to spread. Maybe they even designed a pseudo-vaccine or other medicine to take out survivors.

Or A Plague can be an agent of chaos. When so many are suffering, their defenses are down. This opens the door for malevolent forces to assume control and take advantage of vulnerable people.

From a story standpoint, A Plague is a catalyst for change in your characters. How they handle that change, and particularly how they fight back, will propel your story forward.

"I Heard a Rumor about How This Started"

SCENARIO

Your protagonist is hearing whispers and rumblings about the beginnings of the Plague. It's becoming clear that the government lied to everyone, but the extent of those lies isn't known yet. Did they create the Plague themselves, as a means of population control? Did they know about the Plague but try to hide it from the masses, allowing it to spread and cause more deaths? And who does "they" refer to, exactly? How deep does this conspiracy go?

BRAINSTORM

Think about how quickly a rumor can spread. Who shared these rumors with your protagonist in the first place? And who told *them*, and so on? Map out the chain of events that led to the moment these stories finally got to your protagonist, like a twisted game of telephone. Think about how truthful the rumors might be and in what ways they've mutated over time.

WRITE

Your protagonist works in government. He knows some of the people rumored to be part of this conspiracy and doesn't want to believe what people are saying about them. Write a scene where he questions one of his coworkers and catches her in a lie. Has your protagonist been naive this entire time? Think of this scene as the turning point where your protagonist is radicalized.

Remember: If his coworker is guilty, she may have used your protagonist to help cover up her misdeeds. Does that make your protagonist guilty, even if he only helped inadvertently? Should he be worried about his own safety?

OPTIONAL ELEMENTS TO INCLUDE

- ✖ An overheard conversation.
- ✖ A bribe.
- ✖ Your protagonist discreetly leaves work early.

DYSTOPIAN TWIST

Once a rumor starts, it's difficult to keep it from morphing. What if your protagonist receives word from a friend that she heard another rumor: "People are saying you're involved." Your protagonist had nothing to do with this Plague, but will people believe him? Should he fight this nonsense, or is it smarter to run (even though running would only make him look more guilty)?

“Stay Away from Me”

SCENARIO

A rapidly spreading Plague is causing one of the following epidemics: Everyone is becoming stupid; people are aging quickly (in either direction); or children are turning into aggressive animals. (Feel free to come up with another terrifying outcome of your choice.) Fear is rampant because no one knows exactly how the Plague spreads. But one thing is certain: There is no cure.

BRAINSTORM

Who is your protagonist most afraid of losing? Think about her relationship with this loved one and how deeply connected they are. What difficult trials have they already been through together? What vows have they made? What future have they always envisioned for each other? How much pain would your protagonist feel if she had to betray this person? Could she ever forgive herself?

WRITE

Your protagonist’s loved one has been exposed to the virus. Write a scene where they ask your protagonist for help. The loved one might be freaked out, upset, afraid, worried—or a mixture of all these emotions. But your protagonist is freaked out too. Write a scene where she lets her fear win. Think about what she might say or do to her loved one, and how she might try to avoid helping them.

Remember: Even if your protagonist does a bad thing in this scene, that doesn’t mean she’s a bad person. Show your readers how complicated she is. Is it a mistake to take care of yourself in a situation like this, even if it means doing something hurtful?

OPTIONAL ELEMENTS TO INCLUDE

- An aborted embrace.
- One of the characters sobs uncontrollably.
- The word “please” is repeated several times.

CALLBACKS

Whatever your protagonist decides to do, it's going to hit her loved one hard. What if the loved one doesn't let her off the hook easily? What if the loved one stands firm, demanding your protagonist honor her familial obligation? Think about how deeply you can twist the screws. Make it a decision your protagonist will have a hard time ever moving past.

"They Destroyed the Antidote"

SCENARIO

A terrible Plague has wiped out half the population. Pockets of scientists, researchers, and medical experts are using their minimal resources to search for a cure. Word has begun to spread: Someone out west has created an antidote that works!

BRAINSTORM

If your protagonist found out the cure to all his problems was out of reach—perhaps locked in a safe or stored in a heavily guarded, restricted area—what extreme actions would he take to secure the cure?

WRITE

Write a scene where your protagonist arrives at the medical facility that's rumored to have the antidote he desperately needs. But when he gets there, he discovers he's too late. The antidote has been destroyed. Who would do such a thing, and why? And what desperate actions does this devastating turn of events drive your protagonist to take?

OPTIONAL ELEMENTS TO INCLUDE

- A fire.
- Gunshots in the distance.
- Toxic fumes.

DYSTOPIAN TWIST

What if there never was an antidote to begin with? What if news of the antidote was made up to give people false hope? What if it's all just rumors, lies, and fake news? Would your protagonist survive the hopelessness this revelation might lead to?

Quick Writes

Set a timer for 15 minutes and do not stop writing until the timer goes off. Do not edit, cross out, or censor yourself. Write down every thought that comes to you.

1. Your protagonist has been sheltering in place with a small group. Write a scene where they all finally go outside, and the group is surprised by what they find waiting for them.
2. An awful Plague is spreading. It doesn't kill you; it changes you in a strange, scary way. Write a scene where your protagonist tries to physically outrun this impending disaster.
3. Your protagonist lost several loved ones during the last Plague. Write a scene where he tries to warn people that a new wave of the Plague is coming, but no one believes him.
4. Write a scene where your antagonist deletes a file containing years of research that would help prevent an advancing epidemic. What does your protagonist do when he finds out?
5. Your protagonist has been quarantined in a stadium or convention center. Write a scene where she discovers someone in their shelter is sick. Does she notify others and potentially cause a stampede? Or does she discreetly sneak out and just save her loved ones?

AT A CROSSROADS

It's something your readers will be waiting for, and they'll lean in when it happens. There will be a moment in your story when your protagonist faces a metaphorical fork in the road. Whatever he decides to do At a Crossroads will affect the rest of his journey. It may even define who he is.

Your protagonist might try to convince himself it's better to live within an oppressive system, under the radar. After all, the path of least resistance is easy to follow. Who says he needs to be a hero? But then something pushes him too far, and he realizes the consequences of giving in. He cannot accept a fate determined by his oppressors. Standing up to them isn't just right, it's essential.

This is a significant turning point for your protagonist. He cannot return to being a complacent Cog in the Machine once he's made this costly choice. Even if he doesn't think of himself as a hero, he will have to find the hero within.

As a writer, there may be a time when you reach your own crossroads, debating if you should finish your book. You fear it isn't good enough, but you must find the courage to go on because it's important to you. One way to get past your fear is to put your protagonist At a Crossroads. He's scared but determined to move forward and make a difference. Let him show your readers—and remind you—how it's done.

“What If We Never Find Each Other Again?”

SCENARIO

Your protagonist committed a dangerous and public act of vandalism to expose a corrupt senator's hypocrisy (for example, maybe the representative is leading a campaign against sex workers while secretly hiring them nightly), and now he's being hunted by the government. His face is on posters plastered on street corners. Grainy security footage of him fleeing the senator's home plays in heavy rotation on every news program. Everyone knows his face, so he isn't safe anywhere. He must go into hiding to avoid getting caught.

BRAINSTORM

What was your protagonist's original plan and what complications did he face? Did he have to improvise anything at the last moment? How did it ultimately turn out? How would he rate his success? Get into his head so you have a clear understanding of his emotional state in the aftermath of his dangerous act.

WRITE

Write a scene where your protagonist says goodbye to a loved one before leaving their home forever. He can't tell her where he's going to hide; what if someone came after her for that knowledge? No, he won't put her at risk. And he won't let her join him either, despite how desperately she wants to. Again, it's too risky. What promises do they make to each other? Are they able to express everything they want to say?

Remember: The last thing your protagonist wants to do is leave his loved one. But he has no other choice. Or does he? What if he stayed? Is there any way he could hide here? Don't let his loved one give up on him—let her be the one who makes it clear he's At a Crossroads. Their love for each other will be the thing that makes this decision so impossible.

OPTIONAL ELEMENTS TO INCLUDE

- A knock at the door.
- A wrapped gift.
- A lie.

CALLBACKS

If your protagonist chooses to leave, is there anything his loved one could give him to remind him of her? Think of this as a talisman that will always bring him back to their relationship. Every time he looks at, or holds, this object, it will give him the power to keep going.

"Nobody Crosses This Line Without Making a Sacrifice"

SCENARIO

Your protagonist keeps seeing ads for a fancy new medical procedure that promises to change a person's life. The ads are so ridiculous it's hard to believe they're real. (You decide what kind of change they guarantee—the more outrageous and deranged, the better. It might be something like feline features to help you get in touch with your inner animal, or perhaps the removal of one of your senses to help heighten the remaining ones, or maybe even an operation that somehow makes life in dystopia less depressing.) Your protagonist thought she would have her life together by now, but nothing ever seems to go her way. And every time she sees these ads, she gets more intrigued. Maybe it's worth investigating?

BRAINSTORM

What does your protagonist hate most about herself? What does she wish she could change about her body? What does she wish she could change about her mind? Write a journal entry in her voice where she confesses her most unhinged and vulnerable self-doubts.

WRITE

Write a scene where your protagonist signs up for this "life-changing" medical procedure and is forced to undergo a psychological exam to determine if she's an appropriate candidate. The questions range from innocuous to offensive. Build to a point where your protagonist wants to leave—and maybe she does. Include a moment where payment is discussed, and your protagonist discovers that those performing the procedure don't want money. Whatever type of payment they ask for, make it personal—something that feels more costly than any amount of cash.

Remember: There's no turning back if your protagonist proceeds with this procedure. She is At a Crossroads. Her life will always be broken into two moments: before this procedure and after. Think about how much she's risking here.

OPTIONAL ELEMENTS TO INCLUDE

- Blood work.
- A convoluted form to fill out.
- Anesthesia.

DYSTOPIAN TWIST

Your protagonist has fallen into a trap—perhaps the surgeon has been ordered by the government to secretly implant a device to track citizens' movements or read their minds. Your protagonist knows this operation is shady, but that doesn't necessarily stop her from proceeding. What warning signs does she miss in the doctor's office? Has she told anyone about her appointment, or did she come in secret? Is there a clear moment when she ignores a bad gut feeling?

“It’s Not Safe to Go West”

SCENARIO

Your protagonist is part of a group of refugees on the run from a gang that wants to sell their organs on the black market. Everyone is tired, hungry, and emotional. Tensions are higher than they’ve ever been. Then, after a long day of walking, they reach a literal crossroads. This will not be an easy decision.

BRAINSTORM

What are the complicated dynamics within the group? Think about who your protagonist likes and who he trusts—those categories don’t have to necessarily coincide.

WRITE

Write a scene where the group argues over which road they should take, and they end up splitting into two smaller factions. They debate the pros and cons of each direction. Your protagonist is unsure which one is best, but he will have to make a choice before the sun comes up.

OPTIONAL ELEMENTS TO INCLUDE

- ✖ Your protagonist needs medical care.
- ✖ Two characters come to blows.
- ✖ A prayer.

DYSTOPIAN TWIST

What if there’s a saboteur in the group? What if one of the refugees secretly argues for the path of most resistance? She knows the way to danger and wants to lead them there.

Quick Writes

Set a timer for 15 minutes and do not stop writing until the timer goes off. Do not edit, cross out, or censor yourself. Write down every thought that comes to you.

1. Your protagonist witnesses a significant act of corruption. On his way to report what he saw, a mysterious stranger asks to meet with him in private. Write a scene where this stranger offers your protagonist a case full of money in exchange for his silence.
2. Your protagonist is about to head to a country where he will be free, but it means leaving behind loved ones who are in danger. Does he take the easy exit or fight for his people? Write a scene where he makes the wrong choice, then tries to undo his mistake.
3. Write a scene where your protagonist is asked to choose between two allies who are splitting off into different factions. Make the decision so difficult that he has a mental breakdown.
4. Your protagonist is scouted to work at a corporation that's as evil as it gets. Write a scene where she either accepts or rejects this new job, and she faces immediate consequences for her decision.
5. Your protagonist has printed pamphlets and posters advancing the causes of the Underground Rebellion. She'll be branded a traitor if the government finds out she produced these materials. Write a scene where she considers backing off. What does she ultimately do?

WORST-CASE SCENARIO

Just when you think something bad can't get worse, it becomes the nightmare your protagonist was hoping he'd never encounter. The only good thing about a Worst-Case Scenario is that it gives your protagonist a chance to show what he's made of.

Now you, as a writer, get to ask: "How can I raise the stakes even higher? How can I make an already unbearably tense situation even more dangerous? What is my protagonist's breaking point, and how can I push him to the edge without destroying him?"

The action in dystopian fiction already starts at a heightened place. Use a Worst-Case Scenario to take your story from 60 to 100 miles per hour. Play around with these possibilities:

- ✖ The landscape of your story has been catastrophically altered by climate change. Your protagonist witnesses (or causes) an event that will push the planet past the tipping point.
- ✖ The world of your story has been forever changed by a series of pandemics. There's no way humanity can survive another one. Unfortunately, your protagonist just discovered a brand-new plague.
- ✖ The characters in your story live under a totalitarian regime. Your protagonist helps a group of rebels stage a political coup. But when his friends take power, he realizes they're worse than the totalitarians.

When things go from bad to worse, they might get better. But when they go from bad to Worst-Case Scenario, readers know it's time to brace for dystopia's darkest hour. Let the games begin.

“You’re Not Going to Like This”

SCENARIO

Your protagonist works for an environmental protection group. Things have been getting bad for a while, but they’ve always had emergency procedures to follow. Until now. Your protagonist receives a report that confirms an Earth-ending event will take place in the near future. It’s still possible to save some people, but they would have to believe him first.

BRAINSTORM

What is your protagonist’s specific expertise? Spend some time researching what goes into his job, using as many data-driven resources as possible. (Avoid generative services such as ChatGPT; stick to the kinds of sources your protagonist would trust and use.)

WRITE

Write a series of short scenes where your protagonist tries to convince people in authority that the impending event is catastrophic, but no one cares. They gaslight him and say he’s wrong. They condescend to him. They even threaten him with violence if he continues to spread “lies” and scare people. But your protagonist isn’t fearmongering. Does anyone believe him?

Remember: Your protagonist has allies who believe him—they just might not have enough power to get the message to a significant number of people. But what if they join forces? Would it be possible for them to amplify this message through underground channels, or is it truly hopeless?

OPTIONAL ELEMENTS TO INCLUDE

- Your protagonist is suffering from an unknown illness.
- An explosion in the distance.
- An unexpressed regret.

DYSTOPIAN TWIST

What if this isn't the first time your protagonist has tried to raise an alarm like this? What if no one believes him because he was wrong last time? Could this be a boy-who-cried-Worst-Case-Scenario situation? If so, how tragic would it be if he really did get it right this time?

“Every Time I Think It Can’t Get Worse, It Does”

SCENARIO

A series of losses and tragedies has culminated in your protagonist’s hospitalization. She doesn’t see how today could get any worse. Maybe she even feels a little hopeful now because her luck can only get better from here. Then she hears two doctors discussing an alarming uptick in flu cases. And it isn’t your normal flu; it’s a strange and unusual virus with aggressive symptoms. From what they can tell, it looks like the beginning of a new pandemic. Dammit.

BRAINSTORM

How many pandemics has your protagonist already suffered through? Come up with a brief health timeline for the world of your story, mapping out the most aggressive scares this society has faced. Think about how beaten down people can get when they face multiple catastrophes of this scale within a short period of time.

WRITE

Write a scene where your protagonist tries to get out of the hospital and away from all the sickness around her—but the harder she works to get out, the more impossible escape feels. Throw as many obstacles in her way as you can. Lean into the perverse and the surreal.

Remember: Your protagonist is down but not out; she understands the hospital isn’t the safest place to be, and she will use every resource at her disposal to get to safety. The only question is: *Will it be enough?*

OPTIONAL ELEMENTS TO INCLUDE

- ✖ An alarm goes off.
- ✖ Deep-seated resentment.
- ✖ A message from a dead loved one.

DYSTOPIAN TWIST

What if it isn't an accident that your protagonist ended up at this hospital on the brink of a major epidemic? What if she was chosen by someone who manipulated the chain of events that led her here? What if this malevolent force wants her to get sick?

"I Only Need Five More Minutes"

SCENARIO

Your protagonist is working with a group of underground rebels. They're planning to stage a big demonstration downtown to stand up against a litany of injustices, such as the government's decision to shut down all the schools, a segregation program being instituted in major cities, and a national ban on antidepressants. Just before they leave, your protagonist discovers this is a setup. His so-called allies are the enemy in disguise.

BRAINSTORM

Your protagonist feels like an idiot. Think about how these traitors were able to manipulate him and convince him they were his friends. Have they said or done anything he might be able to use against them now that he knows the truth?

WRITE

Write a scene where your protagonist locks himself in a room and tells the rest of the group he will join them shortly. Now he needs to come up with a plan, and quick. How can he break away from the rest of the group without them realizing he knows who they really are?

OPTIONAL ELEMENTS TO INCLUDE

- A broken lock.
- Sleeping pills.
- A blood oath.

DYSTOPIAN TWIST

Can you double-cross a double-crosser? This is your protagonist's Worst-Case Scenario. Could he then turn the tables and make his false allies face their Worst-Case Scenario?

Quick Writes

Set a timer for 15 minutes and do not stop writing until the timer goes off. Do not edit, cross out, or censor yourself. Write down every thought that comes to you.

1. Write a scene where your protagonist smuggles a mildly contraband substance (such as medicine) across the border. Bad scenario: He gets caught. Worst-Case Scenario: Border control swaps out his meds with something that carries a harsher punishment (such as books).
2. Write a scene where your protagonist gets trapped in a self-driving AI-powered vehicle. Bad scenario: The vehicle is out of control. Worst-Case Scenario: The vehicle is aware of your protagonist's feelings about AI and plans to kill him.
3. Your protagonist has been arrested for a crime she didn't commit. Write a scene where she gets interrogated by the prosecution. Bad scenario: They make her look bad. Worst-Case Scenario: Somehow, your protagonist incriminates herself in multiple other crimes, even though she's innocent.
4. Write a scene where your protagonist fights with a neighbor. Bad scenario: She spars with him over property lines. Worst-Case Scenario: She discovers he's a disgraced dictator from a fallen fascist country; now that he's been identified, he wants her dead.
5. Your protagonist has penetrated enemy lines. Write a scene where he pretends to be an android to avoid capture by military soldiers. Bad scenario: Another android turns him in. Worst Case-Scenario: A group of androids take him hostage and torture him.

STATUS SYMBOLS

Social hierarchies exist to keep people in their place—if everyone has power, no one has power. How would anyone know what a glorious privilege it is to be a member of the elite class if you couldn't compare the "richies" to the hungry, impoverished masses at the bottom of the human food chain?

These distinctions get even more extreme in dystopian times. A caste system makes it easy for those in power to divide society into the worthy and the worthless, giving special privileges to the strong or rich and making life harder for the weak or poor. In your dystopian fiction, consider using Status Symbols to clarify distinctions like these. Think of Status Symbols as a code that quickly communicates where your characters stand in the social hierarchy.

What clothes represent wealth? What car does an elite drive? What products would you find in a lowly person's home? When someone wears a sweater indicating they went to an expensive university, what is she trying to tell people? What does a diamond necklace mean? These objects all act as a visual shorthand. They immediately tell your readers who has all the power and who might have to fight against those factions to survive an unjust system.

What Status Symbols does your protagonist possess, and what do they reveal about her? Perhaps more important, what does she need to acquire to gain social status, and what will she do when she reaches a higher level?

"I Promise to Come Back for You"

SCENARIO

Your protagonist's mother is in serious trouble. Here are some possibilities: She fell victim to identity fraud and the government thinks she's dead; she was apprehended by a border patrol agent and now she's stuck in a detention center; her brain was hacked and she is being pursued by the authorities for a thought crime; or she has been selected for mandatory participation in an infectious disease study where individuals are exposed to dangerous viruses.

BRAINSTORM

Explore your protagonist's relationship with his mother. Come up with five moments from their relationship when she risked her own health and safety to provide for him. If their roles were reversed, what would she do in this situation? In what ways is your protagonist like his mother and how do they differ? What advice might she give him now, if she could?

WRITE

Your protagonist is determined to save his mother, but his current position in society makes him powerless. To save her, he will need more status, or at least the appearance of more status. Write a scene where he illegally acquires an expensive Status Symbol. Make this an extremely difficult task. Perhaps he is forced to make a great personal sacrifice.

Remember: Nothing comes easily in a dystopian world. Think about the possible repercussions of your protagonist's actions. What if he triggers a chain of events that ultimately makes his mother's situation even worse?

OPTIONAL ELEMENTS TO INCLUDE

- ✖ A censored message from his mother.
- ✖ Bloodstained clothes.
- ✖ An act of coercion.

CALLBACKS

Does your protagonist have any inside jokes with his mother, or is there something she always used to say to him when he was feeling low? Think of a phrase he associates with her and then include a moment where a stranger uses this phrase. Your protagonist sees it as a sign that his mother is with him in some way, and that he is on the right path to save her. Let these words motivate him to do whatever it takes to boost his status.

"He Thinks He's Better Than Me Now"

SCENARIO

People are divided into different classes determined by qualities such as intelligence scores and health tests. Citizens are tested annually, and their class shifts up or down, or stays steady, depending on their results. Lower classes must settle for lower standards of living, while those deemed smarter and healthier enjoy more freedom and comfort.

BRAINSTORM

Think about how this kind of society might encourage transactional relationships. How do people in different social classes use each other to get things they need?

WRITE

A couple gets their test results back. Your protagonist discovers he's being promoted, while his girlfriend is staying put in a lower class. Write a scene where the girlfriend complains to a friend about a Status Symbol her boyfriend has acquired. She's jealous and can't let it go. What might she do to ruin his good fortune and bring him back down to her level?

OPTIONAL ELEMENTS TO INCLUDE

A wad of cash, a hurtful lie, or seduction.

DYSTOPIAN TWIST

What if the consequence of cheating on these health and intelligence tests is death? Would your protagonist's girlfriend rather see him die with her than thrive without her? Are people in the lower class leading such miserable lives that the threat of death doesn't stop them from cheating?

“You’re Wearing the Wrong Tag”

SCENARIO

Your protagonist lives in standardized housing reserved for the poorest classes: no frills, no color, no amenities, no joy. Everything in her life has a function; she has no money to waste on anything one might do for pleasure or self-care. But then one day she sneaks into an elite club and sees how much better the upper classes have it. She takes advantage of the open bar. She enjoys the spa amenities. Maybe she even attends a special event in the literature wing, listening to a renowned author discuss his creative process. But then she’s approached by a guard with an electronic scanner, and she’s suddenly exposed as an interloper.

BRAINSTORM

Compare the life your protagonist is used to living with the life she gets to witness inside this club. Is this what she really desires, and if so, why does she want it so badly? And how does this small glimpse of “how the other half lives” change her?

WRITE

Write a scene where your protagonist gets caught socializing among a class of people she’s not supposed to interact with. Make the repercussions swift and firm. Think about how the elites might react to having this low-status character invade their space. Do they make her endure a demeaning body search before she’s allowed to leave? Then what? Do they arrest her? Or do they subject her to an even worse fate?

Remember: Before your protagonist gets caught, she tries to fit in by role-playing as someone who belongs there. What elite ritual does she get wrong that tips off the guards to the fact she is out of place? What Status Symbol does she misappropriate?

OPTIONAL ELEMENTS TO INCLUDE

- ✖ Your protagonist uses an improper word.
- ✖ A delicious treat.
- ✖ A woman screams.

DYSTOPIAN TWIST

At first, this club appears perfect. Your protagonist enjoys herself until she starts to see some of the club's hidden imperfections. What cruel injustices are perpetrated on the low-status people who work here? And do any of the workers recognize her before she gets caught? What do they think about her enjoying the club's special pleasures? Are they happy for her or do they see it as a betrayal?

Quick Writes

Set a timer for 15 minutes and do not stop writing until the timer goes off. Do not edit, cross out, or censor yourself. Write down every thought that comes to you.

1. Your protagonist is having an affair with someone in the upper class. Write a scene where he tells her secrets about a powerful figure who attended his elite college. How can she use this information to help her lower-class family raise their status?
2. Your protagonist discovers a package on his doorstep addressed to him. No return address. Inside, he finds an object that provides access to the upper level of society. But what's the catch?
3. Write a scene where your protagonist learns she has inherited a dangerous gift from a higher-status character.
4. Write a scene where your protagonist steals a uniform from the dead body of a higher-status character. Can he get away with wearing this uniform? How does he avoid getting caught?
5. Write a scene where your protagonist witnesses a higher-class character get murdered. He could go to the authorities, unless . . . What if he could leverage this information in some way? Can he use it to secure more status for himself?

THE CHOSEN ONE

Heroism isn't on your protagonist's to-do list. Dear God, no. The last thing he wants to do is save the day. Who has time for that? Besides, that isn't who he is. All he wants is to lead a quiet, normal life. Unfortunately, that's getting more difficult every day. He hears about food shortages on the news—not normal. He talks to a neighbor about all the deportations in their area—not normal. His friend gets arrested for criticizing the government on social media—not normal. And with every new horror, his innate sense of justice gets triggered. He doesn't want to be a hero, dammit. But no one else seems to be taking this on, and someone's gotta fix this mess. So, he steps up.

There are two ways your protagonist might get selected as The Chosen One. Either he's chosen by others because of his natural leadership skills and strength of character, or he chooses himself because no one else has the courage to do the job.

In both scenarios, there's a feeling that destiny is somehow involved. This goes beyond a sense of duty. Your protagonist was made for this moment, even if he doesn't know it. And maybe his reluctance is a good thing—if he was cockier, he might get everyone killed. Overthrowing an oppressive regime isn't something you can just jump into. It requires patience, smarts, and a stubborn desire to be done with this nonsense and return to a life of normalcy.

“I Have to Do This Alone”

SCENARIO

One of your protagonist’s loved ones desperately needs a specific medication to survive. When a letter from the insurance company denies coverage, your protagonist investigates. He calls a seemingly endless number of times, but none of the bots he talks to can help. Finally, he learns there is a massive shortage of this medication. He’s already lost a sibling and a parent because of the faulty healthcare system. Which is why he seeks out the medication through an illegal underground market. Even though your protagonist himself is beginning to get sick from the radioactivity in the air and soil, he refuses to lose another loved one. He will do anything to keep her alive.

BRAINSTORM

Write a brief history of your protagonist’s relationship with this loved one. Think of one time when she helped him, one lesson she taught him, a few inside jokes they share, one time they experienced great joy together, and one time they suffered through a harrowing loss together. What object reminds him of her? What words or phrases make him think of her? Are there any scents or sounds that trigger memories of times they’ve spent together?

WRITE

Your protagonist comes up with a plan to illegally obtain a large stock of the meds his loved one needs. Write a scene where he tells her what he’s about to do, and she asks to go with him. He knows she’s in no shape to go, but she’s adamant about wanting to help. Does he gently but firmly say no, or does he let her come with him?

Remember: Your protagonist and his loved one are close. She knows she will slow him down if she goes with him, but she also knows he’ll be more willing to put himself in danger if he goes alone. Is it possible her calming presence on this risky mission could be a good thing?

OPTIONAL ELEMENTS TO INCLUDE

- ✖ A gun.
- ✖ A knife.
- ✖ A rope.

DYSTOPIAN TWIST

What if there isn't a shortage of medication? What if the insurance company only says that because they're hoarding supplies for rich people? They don't care if the poor suffer and die. The insurance companies don't profit enough off the poor to make them worth the effort.

“We’re Stronger When We’re Together”

SCENARIO

A ragtag group of insurgents follows a seedy politician on the election trail, staging a series of guerrilla protests at all his speaking events. This man takes great joy in hurting his constituents by restricting their freedom, reducing their resources, and denying them access to public services that provide safety and comfort. But his followers are so brainwashed that they cheer every hateful thing he says. The worse he behaves, the more they seem to love him. The insurgents make a lot of noise and create a big scene every time they protest, but their message is muddy and unfocused—which is why they aren’t getting the traction they hoped for. Nothing they do makes a difference. This leads to rancor and infighting within the group. Maybe they should give up?

BRAINSTORM

What are the details surrounding each of their protests? What do they wear? What do they chant? If you were running a meeting to prep for an upcoming protest, what would be on the agenda?

WRITE

Your protagonist knows the group can make a big difference if they just get their act together. Write a scene where she makes an impassioned speech to the rebels, urging them to stay the course and keep fighting. She lays out a cohesive plan for their next protest. As she talks, she transforms before everyone’s eyes into the leader she was born to be. From this moment forward, everyone in the group will look to your protagonist for guidance. They have chosen her now. She is the leader they need.

Remember: Your protagonist was born for this. The role of leader fits her like a glove. Think about all the ways you can show her stepping into this role with ease.

OPTIONAL ELEMENTS TO INCLUDE

- A rally cry.
- Blueprints laid out on a table.
- A whispered wish.

DYSTOPIAN TWIST

What if there's one other person in the group who wishes he was a natural born leader. Sure, he didn't step up in the first place, but he still thinks he's better suited for the job. If no one else sees that, they don't deserve him. He will do everything he can to sabotage their next protest.

"I Can Feel Our Victory Coming"

SCENARIO

The electricity was out for years. The city finally got its power back, but with a catch: Certain citizens are required to walk on treadmills for an allotted period every night to keep the lights on. The walkers are tired, hungry, and hopeless. It isn't fair that they keep the lights on but never get to benefit from their hard work.

BRAINSTORM

Think about all the socioeconomic inequities within this community. How many ways are the walkers being used and abused?

WRITE

Your protagonist works for the city. There are rumors of a revolt among the walkers. Someone from the city must deliver a pep talk to inspire them to walk with more energy. They all draw straws, and your protagonist gets the short one, which means: He is The Chosen One. Write a scene where he talks to the walkers . . . and unexpectedly empathizes with them.

OPTIONAL ELEMENTS TO INCLUDE

- An apology.
- A tearful rant.
- Blood.

DYSTOPIAN TWIST

What if the treadmills aren't connected to the electricity at all? The only reason the city wants the walkers to walk is to keep them weak and downtrodden.

Quick Writes

Set a timer for 15 minutes and do not stop writing until the timer goes off. Do not edit, cross out, or censor yourself. Write down every thought that comes to you.

1. The elite one-percenters live in elegant private compounds while the poor are crowded together in packed buildings that are falling apart. Write a scene where your protagonist realizes, *There are more of us than there are of them*. He begins to plan a war.
2. It's been over a hundred days since your protagonist got locked up in this detention center for unknown reasons. Write a scene where a group of inmates tell him, "You're the one who has to get us out of here."
3. Write a scene where your protagonist receives a vision from either God or a spirit of some sort, who tells him that he is the only person who can save his dying city.
4. Write a scene where your protagonist stands up to an evil leader and makes a promise: "I will not stop until you've been defeated."
5. A shady government group is rounding up citizens for unspecified reasons. Write a scene where your protagonist decides enough is enough and rallies the citizens to stand up against their attackers.

PROPAGANDA

People tend to believe what they read. The more you hear an idea, the less you question it. That idea lodges itself in your brain. And the more firmly you believe something, the harder it is to unbelieve it—even if that belief is incorrect.

This is how Propaganda works: Misinformation is spread by government leaders—often in a catchy, compelling way—to sway citizens to a certain point of view. There's nothing subtle about Propaganda. It's big and bold. Yet it works subliminally, which is what makes it so pernicious.

That billboard you drive past every day, that news program on the TV at your local bar, that advertisement you see on your retinal scanner news feed—you're so used to these forms of communication you don't notice them anymore. So, when they hit you with the same false information again and again, you forget where you heard it and begin to think it's an original thought. And your original thoughts must be true, right?

Your protagonist is one of the rare citizens who sees through Propaganda. He knows how fast misinformation spreads and how dangerous it is, and he's determined to fight it by enlightening as many people as possible. Or maybe your protagonist finds a clever way to get the truth out by creating his own Propaganda with hidden messages. Have fun figuring out how to subvert or destroy the Propaganda machine and bring the light of truth into your dystopian world.

"Work Is Love"

SCENARIO

Your protagonist works for the government office that produces Propaganda. He might have any job, from working as a designer to operating the printing machines to plastering posters on walls throughout the city. He is a Cog in the Machine who doesn't question what he's doing. Until one of his coworkers—another cog also loving it there—doesn't show up for work one day. Not only that, but their office has been packed up and all evidence of their existence has been removed. This doesn't seem right to your protagonist, but no one else is even remotely concerned. Which makes him even more suspicious . . .

BRAINSTORM

Map out your protagonist's relationship with this coworker. How did they meet, and what did they first bond over? Was their relationship confined to work, or did they spend time together after hours? How much of their personal lives did they share with each other? Do they have any enemies?

WRITE

Write a series of scenes where your protagonist investigates his coworker's disappearance. He is given a generic story from the higher-ups—but the more he learns, the less things add up. He discovers his coworker knew something dangerous, and all these questions might put your protagonist in danger as well.

Remember: Your protagonist is an integral part of the Propaganda machine. He understands how to use this powerful tool. Can he use his skills to deliver a secret message to his lost friend?

OPTIONAL ELEMENTS TO INCLUDE

- ✖ A rabid dog.
- ✖ Someone who refuses to speak to your protagonist.
- ✖ An upsetting photograph.

DYSTOPIAN TWIST

People ask questions about people who ask questions. What if your protagonist discovers that a mysterious stranger is following him around, trying to determine what he's up to?

CALLBACKS

Your protagonist has always believed the Propaganda he preaches. Now that his eyes are open, he might take stock of his past and examine the harmful Propaganda he helped make. How do these memories come back to haunt him now that he can see them in a new light?

"Why Would Anyone Lie to Us?"

SCENARIO

Propaganda is everywhere. Not just on newscasts and billboards. People sell empty space on their skin for tattoos that spread the government's lies. Messages are transmitted subliminally through airwaves. Sleeping citizens download pro-government agendas directly through their dreams. No one remembers a time when they weren't being bombarded with slogans and jargon and ubiquitous advertisements. It's as if everyone forgot how to think for themselves.

BRAINSTORM

Come up with at least five new and unusual ways your protagonist might receive Propaganda. How can you inundate all the characters in your story with so much information that they become numb to it?

WRITE

Write a scene where your protagonist sees something he shouldn't see—a crack in the otherwise pristine landscape of Propaganda. Cracks get bigger when they remain unrepaired. Your protagonist now suspects he's being lied to. Send him down a wild path of revelations and discovery. What will he do when he finally sees all the ways he's being deceived by the government?

OPTIONAL ELEMENTS TO INCLUDE

- A virus.
- Someone chases your protagonist down an alley.
- A moment of seduction.

DYSTOPIAN TWIST

Propaganda is so deeply embedded into people's minds that they parrot its messages without even realizing it. Then, after your protagonist has his big revelation, he sees how harmful these slogans are.

“Everyone Needs to Know”

SCENARIO

Your protagonist stages a series of peaceful protests to raise awareness about a brewing disaster that the government doesn't want people to know about. There is a conspiracy theory that the government and the media want civilians to die because thinning out the population means more resources for the survivors. Which might explain why nightly news reports portray the protesters as a violent group with ulterior motives. The protesters are angry: Their message is getting squashed. Can they reframe their protests in a way that ensures the public will realize what's real?

BRAINSTORM

Come up with at least ten possible actions they could take to amplify their concerns. Make each action larger than the last, then consider the effectiveness of each plan. Is bigger always better?

WRITE

Write a scene where your protagonist's group stages a peaceful protest but subverts it in a significant way. Think about how they can use Propaganda to their advantage. Can they hide an urgent call to action within a chant that seems innocuous? Or what if they word their protest signs in a way that tricks the people they're protesting—the only ones who understand the subtext are the ones who need to hear it most. But will this be too little, too late?

Remember: It could be dangerous for your protagonist to be subversive in her protest. If the wrong people figure out what she's doing, she could be arrested and taken in for questioning. Or even worse, they might not bother with the questioning part—they might just lock her up and forget about her. Make it clear that she's aware of this but persists anyway.

OPTIONAL ELEMENTS TO INCLUDE

- ✖ A chant that turns into song.
- ✖ Unexpected violence.
- ✖ Ominous weather.

DYSTOPIAN TWIST

When you imagine a protest, you probably envision a huge crowd of people. But what if there aren't very many members of the resistance left? What if the entire protest only consists of a handful of people? That doesn't mean they can't make a difference, but it'll be harder. And the absence of their comrades only serves to remind them how dire and important their cause is.

Quick Writes

Set a timer for 15 minutes and do not stop writing until the timer goes off. Do not edit, cross out, or censor yourself. Write down every thought that comes to you.

1. Write a scene where your protagonist discovers her brain has been hacked—she is receiving messages from the government downloaded directly into her consciousness.
2. Write a scene where your protagonist gets caught handwriting missing historical facts into a high school textbook. What ramifications must he face?
3. Write a scene where a group of rebels sew hidden messages of truth into the pockets of clothes before they get sent out for distribution at the local thrift store.
4. Your protagonist is horrified to see his face on a poster promoting intolerance and hatred. He doesn't know who did this or why. How does he react? What does he do?
5. Your protagonist overhears a news report at the local bar detailing a protest he attended. The report is wrong. He tries to get everyone's attention to tell them the truth. But people don't want to listen. Write the fight that ensues.

DYSTOPIAN EDICT

Laws are meant to safeguard citizens from abuse. But sometimes it feels like the whole system has been turned upside down, and new laws have been created to hurt the people they were originally meant to keep safe. When laws become agents of control rather than safeguards against oppression, they enter the realm of a Dystopian Edict.

Books are banned, extreme curfews are implemented, individuality is suppressed, free speech is squashed, women's bodies are governed, artistic expression is outlawed, love is turned into a weapon, history is rewritten, protections are stripped away, rights are withdrawn, and so on. Compliance is mandatory and punishments are swift. These laws are all designed to create fear. Instead of laws existing to help individuals thrive within a larger society, they do the opposite.

The politicians enacting these Dystopian Edicts are trying to beat people into submission. The goal is to overwhelm their constituents, to bombard them with such a massive onslaught of orders that the average person couldn't possibly fight back.

Fortunately, your protagonist isn't the average person. Far from it. Your protagonist believes in the human spirit, despite all the signs telling her she should give up. Your protagonist is just getting started.

“They Took Him While We Were Sleeping”

SCENARIO

Your protagonist’s child has broken one of the new edicts. (Some possibilities: It is illegal to have treasonous thoughts; it is illegal to communicate with anyone in the “outsider” class; it is illegal be outdoors after sundown.) Your protagonist notices her child is acting strangely, and he confesses what he did. She says he’ll be fine but makes him promise not to tell anyone else.

BRAINSTORM

Does the child have a history of troublemaking? Has he broken the law before? Does anyone else know he violated this edict—perhaps someone who might turn him in?

WRITE

Write a scene where your protagonist has a normal morning, getting her family ready for the day. But then she discovers her child is gone. From the state of his bedroom, it is evident that he was taken. She is furious that authorities would go this far—he’s just a child—and distraught that her last words to him were a lie and she didn’t even get a chance to say goodbye.

OPTIONAL ELEMENTS TO INCLUDE

- Your protagonist falls to her knees and prays.
- An urgent phone call.
- Your protagonist is charged a “child removal fee” by the city.

DYSTOPIAN TWIST

What if your protagonist secretly turned in her own son to the authorities because she can't feed the rest of her family? She cries because her plan worked, but she hopes he’ll be taken care of in prison.

"How Did That Get There?"

SCENARIO

Your protagonist is a law-abiding citizen. He does what he's told. He's never knowingly broken a law in his life. New edicts come down from the state capital every week, and they all seem designed to cause terror, confusion, and pain. (The cruelty of these edicts is the entire point.) It can be overwhelming trying to stay on top of all these new rules, but your protagonist makes sure he knows and follows the law.

BRAINSTORM

How does your protagonist deal with confrontation? Has he ever unwittingly broken a law? Think about how he might react if he discovered he was being framed for a crime he didn't commit.

WRITE

Write a scene where your protagonist is approached by a patrol officer, who does a routine body search. The officer "finds" a contraband item in his pocket. Your protagonist swears it isn't his. But he quickly realizes his protestations are worthless; this officer has an arrest quota to fill.

OPTIONAL ELEMENTS TO INCLUDE

- ✖ A witness who refuses to speak.
- ✖ Wrist ties.
- ✖ An empty jail cell.

DYSTOPIAN TWIST

The patrol officer didn't choose your protagonist randomly. Your protagonist possesses a quality the government wants to study. Instead of taking him to jail, the officer brings him to a lab.

“You're Going to Get Everyone Killed”

SCENARIO

Reading is illegal. Knowledge is dangerous. The government doesn't want people learning. Book ownership is a treasonous crime that leads to harsh punishments. Most young people don't even know what books are; those who do also know it isn't wise to mention them. Not even in private—you never know who might hear something and report it to authorities.

BRAINSTORM

Examine how society would change without access to books. Aside from the dumbing down of everyday life, what other ripple effects would result? Think about all the ways people take for granted how much life is enriched by reading.

WRITE

Your protagonist lives in a commune-style home with several family members and friends. Write a scene where he discovers a massive secret stash of books that belong to his closest confidante. He confronts his friend about the books, urging her to get rid of them. But she refuses. How does your protagonist handle the situation?

Remember: Your protagonist is old enough to remember books. His reading skills might be a bit rusty, but he knows how. Is he tempted to open these newly discovered treasures?

OPTIONAL ELEMENTS TO INCLUDE

- *Pride and Prejudice* by Jane Austen.
- *Frankenstein* by Mary Shelley.
- *War and Peace* by Leo Tolstoy.

DYSTOPIAN TWIST

Your protagonist is smart enough not to talk to people about how much he misses reading, but he often daydreams about favorite books from childhood. What if this secret stash of books is a trap? What if these books were planted here to test how he would react? The instant he opens a book and starts reading, he fails the test.

Quick Writes

Set a timer for 15 minutes and do not stop writing until the timer goes off. Do not edit, cross out, or censor yourself. Write down every thought that comes to you.

1. An anti-poverty edict makes it illegal for the balance of your bank account to fall below a certain amount. Write a scene where your protagonist gets arrested on the way to make a deposit.
2. An anti-waste and contamination edict makes it illegal to discard or give away food. Write a scene where your protagonist gets arrested for trying to share leftovers with an impoverished neighbor.
3. An anti–air pollution edict makes it illegal to talk in public above a certain decibel. Write a scene where your protagonist gets arrested for talking to a street vendor too loudly.
4. An anti-assembly edict makes it illegal for more than five people to gather at an outdoor space. Write a scene where your protagonist gets arrested for stopping to say hello to a friend who is already part of a small group.
5. An anti-correction edict makes it illegal for anyone to point out when a member of government is wrong about something. Write a scene where your protagonist gets arrested for writing an anonymous op-ed about how the government is failing the people.

MINDLESS DRONE

A Mindless Drone doesn't start that way. This is a supporting character—rebellious and unique, whip-smart, an emotional firecracker—who becomes an ally to your protagonist in their mutual quest for freedom. He is the Cog in the Machine's opposite. Instead of slowly waking up to the horrors around him, a Mindless Drone knows . . . and then slowly forgets.

When your readers meet him, he has hopes, dreams, and goals he's determined to accomplish despite the bleakness around him. He's actively fighting oppression. He questions everything.

Until he can't.

One day something happens that makes him see his life in a new light. Maybe he's threatened, or a loved one is endangered. For the first time, he understands the consequences of rebellion. Maybe living a life filled with meaning and purpose is overrated? Who says compliance is such a bad thing? What made him think it was a good idea to put everyone he loves at risk? Perhaps the only way to truly break free is to accept not having freedom and settle for the status quo.

He's been either brainwashed or beaten down so thoroughly that he can't fight back. Instead of breaking the machine, he willingly becomes a cog. It's a heartbreaking arc. Your readers will ache to see this character embrace the ideas he used to stand up against.

He had dreams, but he learned that dreaming is dangerous. So, he pushed them aside. Work, eat, sleep, repeat.

“You’re Scaring Me”

SCENARIO

Your protagonist has a job helping people at one of the only remaining eco-friendly, ethically conscious companies left. Their competitors are notorious for bribing government officials to turn a blind eye to bad behavior such as mismanagement of hazardous materials, release of pollutants into the air and water supply, and excessive consumption of energy. Your protagonist’s job doesn’t pay well, but it’s emotionally fulfilling. He and his coworkers often talk about how grateful they are for what they do. It’s a small life but a good one, and your protagonist wouldn’t change it for the world. If he has one regret, it would be that he can’t help more people.

BRAINSTORM

Think about what your protagonist has sacrificed to make his current life possible. What creature comforts does he live without? Are his basic needs being met? How might his life be different with more money, better health-care, and total freedom?

WRITE

Your protagonist shows up at work and discovers his closest confidante is gone. He took a better-paying job at a corporation they both actively despise because of its anti-environmental policies. Write a scene where your protagonist tracks down his friend to find out what happened, and he’s shocked by who he finds. This isn’t the friend he’s known and worked with for years. What happened to the caring, principled person he once knew?

Remember: As much as your protagonist thought he and his friend were in alignment, they clearly have different values. Think about how this experience might radicalize your protagonist and make him even more determined to push for justice and help people in need.

OPTIONAL ELEMENTS TO INCLUDE

- ✖ The friend says they were never as close as your protagonist thought they were.
- ✖ A security guard asks the friend if your protagonist is bothering him.
- ✖ A nondescript office building where everyone looks the same.

CALLBACKS

What if your protagonist packs up some of the personal items his friend left behind and brings them along to this meeting? How might the significance of one of these objects help his friend remember the important causes he used to feel so passionate about? Is this really only about money, or is something more sinister going on?

"Don't Lie to Them, I've Always Been Like This"

SCENARIO

Your protagonist's sister disappeared a long time ago. She was a popular influencer who was outspoken in her critiques of the government; then one day, she was just gone. All her videos inexplicably disappeared too. Your protagonist stopped looking for her years ago, when the trail got cold. But sometimes he still thinks he sees her in a crowd.

BRAINSTORM

Think about how memories can fade over time, especially when it comes to the people we've lost. Make a list of everything your protagonist has forgotten about his sister. Has he made up any memories about her that aren't true? Is he a victim of a secret, government-sponsored mass medical experiment to destroy memories and create Mindless Drones?

WRITE

Write a scene where your protagonist bumps into his long-lost sister and she doesn't want to talk to him. Build to an argument about the person he thinks she is versus the person she says she is. Has she been brainwashed?

OPTIONAL ELEMENTS TO INCLUDE

- A crowd of onlookers.
- One of her deleted videos pops back up in an unexpected place.
- A dullness in her eyes.

DYSTOPIAN TWIST

What if the crowd turns on your protagonist? They're all Mindless Drones who think he's here to hurt his sister. If their mob mentality gets out of hand, your protagonist will be in great danger.

"We Need to Talk About Your Daughter"

SCENARIO

Your protagonist and her spouse are concerned about their teenage daughter. There's something off about her new friends at school. She used to think for herself, but now she does what they do, says what they say, and believes what they believe. Also, she seems to be parroting a lot of the cultural talking points from the harsh and controlling fascist media. At first they thought it was normal teen rebellion, then they realized she was supporting an ideology that wants to take her rights away. What's going on here?

BRAINSTORM

Think about the beliefs they tried to instill in their daughter, and the beliefs they've heard her express lately. How could she possibly have strayed so far from what they taught her?

WRITE

Your protagonist and her spouse don't want to think of their daughter as a Mindless Drone. They blame her friends for making her this way. Write a scene where they confront a parent of one of their daughter's friends. This scene could go in a few different directions: The parent is just as concerned about her own daughter and they all bond; the parent blames them for her daughter's new belief system; the parent is also a Mindless Drone who doesn't see anything wrong with what their kids believe. By the end of the scene, your protagonist is more worried than before.

Remember: This isn't really about someone else's daughter; it's about their daughter. All your protagonist wants is for her kid to go back to how she was. But is that possible? If she's been brainwashed, can your protagonist reverse the damage that's been done to her?

OPTIONAL ELEMENTS TO INCLUDE

- A gift.
- Someone gets physically sick.
- Tense silence.

CALLBACKS

Your protagonist might try to remind her daughter what she was taught to believe by listing "good" experiences from her childhood—but none of these memories land the way your protagonist was hoping they would.

Quick Writes

Set a timer for 15 minutes and do not stop writing until the timer goes off. Do not edit, cross out, or censor yourself. Write down every thought that comes to you.

1. Your protagonist's closest ally doesn't show up for an important event. Write a scene where your protagonist goes to his friend's home and his friend claims not to know him.
2. Your protagonist's spouse is cheating on her with a chatbot. Write a scene where she discovers the bot's influence has completely changed her husband's belief system.
3. People are tired of feeling despair. Write a scene where your protagonist tries to stop a loved one from getting a medical procedure that would turn them into a Mindless Drone so they'd no longer feel depressed about the state of the world.
4. It's the first day of your protagonist's new job. Write a scene where she meets her new coworkers and realizes they are all Mindless Drones. Is that her destiny too?
5. At a routine doctor's appointment, your protagonist is unexpectedly subjected to a series of tests. Write a scene where he tries to escape before they can turn him into a Mindless Drone. Does he get out in time?

FORBIDDEN LOVE

You might ask, "Who has time for love when the world is burning?" And then your heart might reply, "If not now, when?"

Two characters who find love in the middle of dystopia aren't doing so out of desperation. They cling to each other because they know love is necessary, and there's nothing an oppressive regime can say or do to tell them otherwise. There's nothing wrong with their love.

Unless it's forbidden, that is. A Forbidden Love puts the parties involved in perilous positions. They're forced to hide their romance because of the danger it poses.

What makes a love forbidden? Perhaps your protagonist has fallen for someone in a different social class. Or maybe she goes on an undercover mission Behind Enemy Lines, where she meets and falls in love with someone who's trying to take away her freedom. Or maybe it has nothing to do with who the other person is but has everything to do with what their love does—perhaps their desire has been poisoned in some way and it's not safe for these two characters to be together.

These romances are often doomed from the beginning. But try telling your protagonist not to follow her heart. She won't stand for it. And neither will your readers.

"We Can't Do This Anymore"

SCENARIO

Your protagonist is in love with a patrol officer who made one of her family members disappear. At first she hated him, but in a cruel twist of fate he now feels like the only connection she still has to her lost loved one. They have secret trysts before and after his shift, whenever they can. If anyone found out, they would both be in trouble. She would be arrested, and he could be killed. They never should have started this in the first place. But when they're together, the rest of the world falls away. Your protagonist would do anything for this man, even though she hates that he works for the evil authorities. (And despite the fact that she fears he might be evil as well.) Is it just passion, or is this love?

BRAINSTORM

Your protagonist hasn't told anyone about her Forbidden Love, but there are subtle signs. Think about the ways her behavior has changed since she started her affair. Does she act differently? Hold herself differently? Dress differently? Speak differently? Has anyone in her life noticed any of these shifts? If her loved ones found out, what would they think? How much danger of exposure is she in right now?

WRITE

Write a scene where your protagonist tries to break up with the patrol officer but she can't go through with it. Set the scene in a public place—chosen by your protagonist to prevent the two of them from getting physical with each other. It's important to have this conversation, and she knows that if they're alone, they might not get any actual talking done.

OPTIONAL ELEMENTS TO INCLUDE

- ✖ A reckless display of affection.
- ✖ A disguise.
- ✖ A recording device.

DYSTOPIAN TWIST

They think they're being so secretive, but what if they're wrong? What if the patrol officer has a body camera embedded in his uniform that records his every action—even his most private moments with your protagonist? What if there is a recording of everything she says to him, words that could be used against her if the government ever wants to make her do their bidding?

"If You Never See Me Again, It's Because They Found Out"

SCENARIO

Your protagonist is one of the bad guys, but in his defense he never knew better. He grew up among fascists and has always believed what they told him to believe. (You decide what makes his family so bad: Maybe they own a major corporation that poisons the environment, or their shady financial dealings have pushed millions into bankruptcy.) But he's fallen in love with a spy who went Behind Enemy Lines—and she has opened his eyes to the cruelty his family has inflicted on the world. He wants to abandon his family and help the masses lead better lives. If only it wasn't so daunting to change his life so drastically.

BRAINSTORM

Explore the roller coaster of emotions your protagonist must have gone through when he realized his beliefs and actions have been hurting people. How difficult is it for him to accept culpability for his actions? Is there still a part of him that's in denial?

WRITE

Write a breakup scene between your protagonist and his Forbidden Love interest. They both suspect that other people know about their relationship, and they're worried about the consequences if the wrong people find out.

Remember: Your protagonist would have to sacrifice a lot—family, money, safety—to do the right thing and denounce his family. Does he have the moral fortitude and strength of character to take such a risk? Is there anyone in his life who would stand by him?

OPTIONAL ELEMENTS TO INCLUDE

- ✖ A torn garment.
- ✖ A sealed envelope, to be opened later.
- ✖ Storm clouds.

DYSTOPIAN TWIST

What punishment would your protagonist consider worse than death? Think about all the things his family might do to him if they found out about his relationship. Then consider: Is there any world in which he defects from his family and finds safety on the outside?

"If You Won't Take My Heart, Take My Life"

SCENARIO

Androids have officially been recognized as citizens and they now have all the same rights as humans do—in fact, they have more rights than some people. They are an inescapable, sometimes deadly, part of society, especially in the human prisons where jailers have been replaced by androids to eliminate human tenderness. Everyone knows at least a few androids—and if you think you don't, you're wrong.

BRAINSTORM

How does an android talk? What specific tells do they have that might give them away in conversation? What words or phrases do they use the most? What are their verbal tics?

WRITE

Your protagonist has been getting increasingly antisocial as she falls in love with an android prison guard. Write a scene where she confesses her undying affection while ignoring messages or calls from a formerly incarcerated flesh-and-blood loved one.

OPTIONAL ELEMENTS TO INCLUDE

- A scream.
- Sleeping pills.
- A shocking moment of tenderness.

DYSTOPIAN TWIST

What if the android's brain is a perfect algorithm designed to say and do everything that makes your protagonist happy—and it was also designed to sell her as many products as possible?

Quick Writes

Set a timer for 15 minutes and do not stop writing until the timer goes off. Do not edit, cross out, or censor yourself. Write down every thought that comes to you.

1. Your protagonist works in either the service or hospitality industry. Through her job, she has a casual flirtation with a powerful political figure. He doesn't seem as evil in person as he does on the news. Write a scene where he asks her out on a date.
2. Love, relationships, and marriage are illegal. Sex is allowed only on a purely transactional basis. Write a scene where your protagonist makes a confession of love to someone who is incapable of keeping a secret.
3. Your protagonist has a crush on a man she's never spoken to because he's in a higher social circle. Write a scene where she crashes an event he will be at—and accidentally learns of plans to dispose of her entire social class.
4. Your protagonist can't pay his rent, and he's scheduled for execution. Write a scene where he tries to seduce the woman in charge of his criminal case. Is he successful? And if so, how does his success complicate his life further?
5. Your protagonist is in love with a dead woman. Write a scene where he does something drastic to try to bring her back to life.

HIGH-STAKES GAME

A life of freedom is full of choices, from the insignificant (*What should I have for breakfast?*) to the deeply meaningful (*What do I want to do with my life?*) and everything in between. An autocratic leader will strip those options away from you, one by one, until you no longer have any decisions to make. You do what you're told, and if you're smart, you pretend to be grateful. But deep down, you yearn for the freedom you once had.

A High-Stakes Game sponsored by the government gives people the illusion of choice. You don't have to participate if you don't want to. But you're desperate, and this High-Stakes Game could be your only way out of the dystopian hellscape you're living in. The government is offering winners a significant amount of money, not to mention perks that would make life easier. Your protagonist knows the High-Stakes Game is most likely rigged but still competes. He must at least try to win a better life for himself.

No matter how prepared your protagonist thinks he is for this High-Stakes Game, he won't be ready. Authoritarians use violence as a means of control, so their game will be full of bloody and savage twists. If your protagonist gets out of this alive, he will finally make the choice he was destined to make: He will decide to overthrow this game and all the people who created it.

“Only One of Us Is Getting Out of Here Alive”

SCENARIO

When you have nothing to live for, you have nothing to lose. So why not participate in a game of survival where only half the competitors get out alive? To solve the problem of overpopulation, cities have begun to sponsor a series of life-or-death physical challenges. And most people figure that a 50 percent chance of winning life-changing money is worth the risk. But what if you meet the love of your life while playing this horrific game? Suddenly the stakes shoot through the roof. Because if only one of you wins, you both still lose.

BRAINSTORM

Think about your protagonist's relationship history. Has he ever been in love before? If not, what kept him from committing? And if he has experienced a great love, is he still reeling from the end of that relationship? How did this loss prepare him for this current moment? How did it shape him? Think of this as painting a portrait of who he is through his romantic entanglements.

WRITE

Your protagonist and his love interest are competing on opposite teams in the next game. Write a scene where they confess their undying love for each other. Which means, wait—they both have to live! But how? Can they bend the rules? Can they trick the judges? Or would it be possible to break the game entirely?

Remember: They just met, but their feelings for each other run deep. Make sure your readers get invested in their relationship. This is an intense situation. With their defenses down, they can get vulnerable with each other quickly. Let your readers see that this relationship was meant to be.

OPTIONAL ELEMENTS TO INCLUDE

- ✖ A first kiss.
- ✖ Encroaching flames.
- ✖ A promise withheld.

DYSTOPIAN TWIST

What if the love interest doesn't love him back? What if she's only faking it to disarm him and make it easier for herself to win? Or what if her love is true, but someone puts this paranoid thought in his head? Is it ever possible to trust someone in a High-Stakes Game?

“We're Running Out of Time!”

SCENARIO

There's no such thing as public education anymore. Education is reserved for the elite classes. Your protagonist wants to participate in a High-Stakes Game because it's the only way she can earn enough money to send her younger siblings to school. Her family is against the risks. As far as she's concerned, the game is the only way they'll have any sort of future. But they're afraid they might have to face that future without her.

BRAINSTORM

Make a list of losses. How much has your protagonist and her family suffered? How badly do they need a win right now?

WRITE

Write a scene where your protagonist makes an impassioned speech to her loved ones to convince them the High-Stakes Game is the best (and possibly only) solution to their problems.

OPTIONAL ELEMENTS TO INCLUDE

- An ultimatum.
- A mask (literal or metaphorical).
- A curse.

DYSTOPIAN TWIST

Anyone can sign up for the games. What if one of your protagonist's loved ones signs up too—and they are forced to compete against each other?

“Shhhhh!”

SCENARIO

Your protagonist is competing in a High-Stakes Game where the ultimate winner gets a seat on an influential political board—a position that comes with life-changing perks. Most of the competitors won't make it out of this game alive. And now that the game has begun, your protagonist realizes his chances of winning are slim. But maybe, just maybe, if he can find a place to hide, the game will end, and he'll get out alive. It's unlikely, but if he can just disappear and stay quiet long enough . . . then he'll have a chance to find another way to take a stand for his long-suffering community.

BRAINSTORM

What are the rules of this game he's engaged in? Have the people in charge come up with a fail-safe to prevent participants from hiding? Do they already know where he is, in which case they're only letting him feel like he's safe? Get inside the heads of the game-makers to understand how they would deal with this situation.

WRITE

Write a scene where your protagonist hides with his closest ally in the game. This could be the end for both, so they bond with each other. Maybe your protagonist shares a secret that's been weighing on him. Maybe the ally shares a memory of someone from his family he'll miss if they never get out of here. Maybe your protagonist expresses a regret about something he never got to do with his life—maybe he wishes he had the strength to just take power from other people so he could bring about change that can only be enacted by the ruling class. But that's not who he is. Let them be vulnerable in what might be their final moments.

Remember: If they get caught, they die. They must remain as quiet as possible, which adds an extra layer of intimacy to their interaction.

OPTIONAL ELEMENTS TO INCLUDE

- ✖ An explosion in the distance.
- ✖ One of them has a scary wound that needs medical care.
- ✖ A rodent.

DYSTOPIAN TWIST

What if your protagonist's ally is dead and all this is happening inside his head? So, in a way, he's really talking to himself. Will he be able to set aside the thoughts that make him weak and find the strength to do whatever it takes to survive?

Quick Writes

Set a timer for 15 minutes and do not stop writing until the timer goes off. Do not edit, cross out, or censor yourself. Write down every thought that comes to you.

1. Your protagonist is debating whether she should participate in a High-Stakes Game. (You decide the rules and stakes.) Write a scene where she plays a mini version of the game to see if she has what it takes to win.
2. Your protagonist won a new life in a High-Stakes Game, but now he has nightmares every night about what he went through. Write a scene where he does something extreme to try to erase his memories.
3. Your protagonist lost everything in a High-Stakes Game—except his life. Write a scene where he asks a stranger to help put his life back together.
4. Write a scene where your protagonist begs an official to let him participate in a High-Stakes Game. He lays himself bare, putting everything on the line.
5. Write a scene where your protagonist leads a protest against an upcoming High-Stakes Game, but she has a secret: She would play the game if she could. In fact, she recently sent in an application.

ACCIDENTAL MURDER

Your protagonist is a good person, but she did a "bad" thing in the eyes of someone in the ruling class. It's possible your protagonist did nothing wrong, but her innocence is incidental. The only thing that matters now is that a powerful person thinks she's guilty of a capital crime and wants justice. So, your protagonist does what she can to survive in this terrible, topsy-turvy world.

At some point in your story, she will find herself cornered or confronted by the person who wants her arrested. She might try to reason with this person. She might turn herself in, if she doesn't see any other options. Or . . .

She might accidentally murder this person.

The thing to remember about the Accidental Murder trope is it's more interesting if it's truly an accident. She didn't expect the gun to go off; she didn't think the rock she hurled at her opponent's head would make contact; she was shocked when her nemesis fell ten stories to his death after what she thought was a harmless shove.

When your protagonist commits an Accidental Murder, it's a delicious turn of the screw for your readers. They will be hooked by the drama of your protagonist's predicament. The stakes couldn't be higher. She committed the worst possible crime, yet she's not guilty. She'll have to be clever to get out of this mess. If she fails, her fatal mistake could have fatal consequences.

Whoops

SCENARIO

Your protagonist has been unlawfully detained in his small town, which was overrun by a gang after the former political leaders were abducted. Now, he's stuck in a prison with others who feel just as lost and hopeless as he does. No one will give him answers or tell him why he's here. The detainees are growing restless. They're tired, hungry, angry, scared. Your protagonist is at the center of everything, making friends and allies. He tells the others he will get answers.

BRAINSTORM

What's your protagonist's plan? Is he going to claim he has powerful friends who are looking for him? Does he think that if he's loud enough, those in power will finally listen? Come up with several tactics. He understands this might be a fruitless endeavor, but he needs to do something.

WRITE

Write a scene where your protagonist corners a surly security guard and demands that he be allowed to make a phone call to loved ones, or have a lawyer represent him, or speak to someone in charge. A crowd might gather as he makes a scene. And then he accidentally murders the guard, in a sudden, ridiculous manner of your choice. Make it so shocking and messed up that your protagonist finds it almost funny at first—until he realizes he's in even more trouble than before.

Remember: Your protagonist has allies here. His new friends don't want him to get in any more trouble than he's already in. What might they do to protect him now that he's committed an actual crime? Is there any way they can dispose of the body without getting caught?

OPTIONAL ELEMENTS TO INCLUDE

- ✖ A security camera that must be destroyed.
- ✖ A giggle fit.
- ✖ A string of curse words.

DYSTOPIAN TWIST

What if the guard doesn't know why he's here either? What if he's a prisoner too? The only difference is, he's been afforded a little more freedom than the rest. Think about how systems of oppression create the illusion of power for people who are being manipulated by the authorities.

"No One's Going to Believe Us"

SCENARIO

Your protagonist's life has been upended by a malicious stalker. He follows her when she least expects it; he messages her constantly; he keeps finding ways to bother her—morning, noon, and night. She reports him at the local police station, but they won't help her—ever since the new regime took office, stalking is no longer considered a crime. She is completely on her own except for one friend, who promises to stay with her until something changes and she feels safe again.

BRAINSTORM

Who is this person terrorizing your protagonist? Maybe she knows him—it could be a neighbor, a coworker, or even a local leader (who is respected but has a dark side). Think about how long this person has been obsessed with your protagonist. How many times has she reported him? How many people know about their conflict? How public has she been about her fears?

WRITE

Write a scene where your protagonist and her friend decide to turn the tables on the stalker. All they want to do is give him a bit of his own medicine. So, they surprise him on his territory. They sneak into his home or private office. Things escalate quickly and they accidentally murder him. It's not self-defense; it just happens. This is when your protagonist's real problems begin: Even if they say it was an accident, no one will believe her because they know about her conflict with this man. She's totally screwed. How does she get out of this?

OPTIONAL ELEMENTS TO INCLUDE

- ✖ A wound that won't stop bleeding.
- ✖ A body in a shallow grave.
- ✖ They've accidentally murdered the wrong stalker.

CALLBACKS

What are the stalker's last words? What if he says something that will haunt your protagonist through the rest of your story? Does he claim to be innocent? Does he say he's been working for someone else? Whatever it is, make it a final statement she won't be able to shake.

"Run!"

SCENARIO

The government has rolled back hundreds of environmental rules. Animals are dying. The water is polluted. Food is filled with toxic substances. Meanwhile, a member of your protagonist's family is sick. Your protagonist escorts his family member to a rally to confront a corrupt leader who voted for deregulation.

BRAINSTORM

Your protagonist has watched his loved one get sicker and sicker. Think through how her illness first presented itself, then chart out how her symptoms progressed. Be as specific as possible. Get in your protagonist's head. How has witnessing this pain changed him?

WRITE

Write a scene where your protagonist and his loved one attend this rally and confront the leader in front of many witnesses. Your protagonist brought a weapon just in case he wants to appear like more of a threat. But he doesn't intend to use it. Then the gun accidentally goes off. Oh no.

OPTIONAL ELEMENTS TO INCLUDE

- ✖ A stampede.
- ✖ A stranger helps them.
- ✖ A moment of absolute silence.

DYSTOPIAN TWIST

What if there aren't very many people at this rally? What if most of the population agrees with these deregulations? What if your protagonist and his loved one are among the select few who haven't been brainwashed into believing they're better off now?

Quick Writes

Set a timer for 15 minutes and do not stop writing until the timer goes off. Do not edit, cross out, or censor yourself. Write down every thought that comes to you.

1. Your protagonist is in a self-driving taxi that malfunctions. Write a scene where he triggers the manual drive fail-safe function just as the car barrels into a crowd, causing mayhem. Your protagonist knows he'll be blamed for this. What does he do now?
2. Write a scene where your protagonist gets into a heated argument with a nasty neighbor or an unscrupulous landlord with whom he has a long, difficult history. A few shoves near a faulty banister cause an unexpected tumble. How's he going to spin this?
3. Your protagonist works late, which means she's out past curfew. She has a prop toy gun she carries for defense. Write a scene where a prickly patrol officer gives her trouble, and she discovers the hard way that the weapon in her purse is real.
4. Write a scene where your protagonist drops a heavy object out her window to try to scare an enemy but the object lands on (and kills) an innocent bystander. Come on, universe!
5. Write a scene where your protagonist confronts an enemy in a factory. A small action—such as a sneeze—distracts the enemy momentarily, causing him to fall into a dangerous machine and die instantly. Your protagonist runs for her life.

NOT WHO THEY SAY THEY ARE

It can be hard to trust people in the best of times. But when the times turn so ugly that you can't trust anyone, who can you turn to?

Your protagonist wants to believe people are basically good. He wants to be a force for positive change. The only way to survive when dystopia drains the life out of once-thriving communities is to keep your humanity intact. Your protagonist understands that you do this through relationships, so he keeps trusting—even though he's been burned before. Every time he meets someone new, he thinks, *Maybe this relationship will work.*

If only life were that easy. The pain your protagonist will feel when he finds out a trusted ally is Not Who They Say They Are will change him forever.

What's that old, hackneyed saying? "You catch more flies with honey than vinegar." Well, it's easier to accomplish an evil agenda if you trick people into believing you're looking out for their best interests. At least that's what the bad actors in dystopia think. They are Not Who They Say They Are, and the repercussions of this could be devastating for your protagonist. But as a writer, you can turn this around; your protagonist can figure out who they really are in time to do damage control. And maybe he can even find someone trustworthy to join the battle.

"I'd Feel Sorry for You If I Didn't Hate You"

SCENARIO

Trust is hard to come by these days. The leader of a doomsday cult has found a way to hack the human brain in an ingenious way that allows him to exert control without any outward change in personality. No one can be sure who has or has not been hijacked by the cult. So, people watch out for themselves. Your protagonist doesn't have many friends, and she rarely allows herself to be unguarded even with the ones she trusts. But then she lets her defenses down and shares a secret with a new friend. Big mistake.

BRAINSTORM

Think through your protagonist's friendship history. Has she ever had a best friend before? How has she been burned by former friends? What emotional walls did she already have in place when she made this new friend, and how did her current confidante break those walls down? Think about what's at stake in this relationship.

WRITE

Write a scene where your protagonist discovers her closest friend has been lying about something important and as she exposes this lie, their entire history together unravels. But here's the kicker: Now that her friend's lies have been revealed, the friend shows her true self, and it's ugly. Does this mean she's one of *them*?

Remember: There's a reason the friend has been lying to your protagonist. Think about what she wants. Has she been spying on your protagonist? Has she been collecting data? What are her ulterior motives? Is she even in control of her own mind?

OPTIONAL ELEMENTS TO INCLUDE

- ✖ A slap in the face.
- ✖ A punched wall.
- ✖ A simple question: "Why?"

DYSTOPIAN TWIST

The friend suspects your protagonist is part of the doomsday cult, and she's determined to find a way to confirm her suspicions. What technological tools might she use? Their close relationship has given her access to every part of your protagonist's life—think about all the sinister ways she could take advantage of this proximity.

"Who's Making You Do This?"

SCENARIO

Your protagonist lives with family and takes care of elderly parents or maybe an ailing sibling. Their politics don't always align, but blood is thicker than party affiliation, right? Not necessarily. All your protagonist's notions about the sanctity of family are about to be shattered.

BRAINSTORM

A senselessly cruel government has begun enslaving citizens who do not meet a certain threshold on mandatory IQ tests. Rumors are rampant that the testing system is rigged, but even if it isn't, it's still a horrific abuse of power. Your protagonist is busy fighting for justice, trying to disrupt the entire system. But he knows not to bring up politics when he comes home to his conservative family for the night. Make a list of ten lies he has told his loved ones about what he's up to. Is he good at keeping his extracurricular activities private, or is it more of an open secret that they've chosen not to address?

WRITE

Write a scene where your protagonist discovers one of his family members has been covertly tracking his every move and sending reports to a particularly nasty official who works at a local government office. Your protagonist doesn't want to believe his family would turn on him. He's desperate to believe they're being coerced or blackmailed; someone must be manipulating them!

Remember: Your protagonist is shocked to discover his family member would do such a thing, but the signs have been there all along. Make this moment feel both surprising and inevitable.

OPTIONAL ELEMENTS TO INCLUDE

- ✖ Your protagonist is taken away in handcuffs.
- ✖ A bitter, ugly rant.
- ✖ Pure hatred.

DYSTOPIAN TWIST

Propaganda. Misinformation. Untruths. They're all buzzwords that mean the same thing: lies. Think about how one lie can infect someone, and how that person can pass the lie on to someone else, and another person, and another, until an entire society is caught up in an epidemic of deceit. How has your protagonist protected himself up to this point? What would happen if he ultimately got infected and fell in line with the rest of his family's beliefs?

“But I Trusted You”

SCENARIO

The sun is dying—soon it will entirely burn out. Maybe that's why everyone seems to be losing their minds. Your protagonist is madly in love. His relationship is the only thing keeping him sane. When he's with her, he can ignore the literal darkness that's taking over the world.

BRAINSTORM

Do some freewriting about how it feels to be in the bubble of love. Think about how much your protagonist has grown to depend on his partner to maintain his sanity. How would he react, both physically and emotionally, if that was suddenly taken from him?

WRITE

Write a scene where your protagonist discovers his partner works for a collective of conspiracy theorists who think climate change is a hoax and have escalated the current crisis. She claims to love him, but everything about what she does goes against his belief system. The people she works for are evil. Is there any way he can move past this betrayal, or is this over forever?

OPTIONAL ELEMENTS TO INCLUDE

- A moment of bargaining.
- An admission of truth that still contains a lie.
- An act of submission.

CALLBACKS

Your protagonist should have seen this coming. There were signs he ignored along the way. What parts of his relationship suddenly take on a different meaning now that he has this new context for who is partner is and what she does?

Quick Writes

Set a timer for 15 minutes and do not stop writing until the timer goes off. Do not edit, cross out, or censor yourself. Write down every thought that comes to you.

1. Your protagonist is developing an artificial seed (or another exciting piece of tech that would have a positive effect on society). Write a scene where she discovers her closest ally at work is an undercover spy who just sabotaged the entire project.
2. Write a scene where your protagonist discovers his closest ally is secretly a rat, cockroach, or other vermin. Don't explain how or why. But make one thing clear: This relationship is poison.
3. Your protagonist bumps into an old friend, and they bond over a mutual fear that they won't survive the current regime. Write a scene where your protagonist discovers her friend works for this regime and is trying to recruit her.
4. A group of survivors are on a long trek to find a rumored utopian city. Write a scene where your protagonist discovers the group's leader has been lying to them: The city doesn't exist. Does your protagonist tell the group or is it better to let them find out for themselves?
5. Your protagonist has been arrested for having optimistic thoughts (or another equally outrageous "crime" that shows how the government is extinguishing resilience). Write a scene where he's being interrogated, and the detective reveals he was turned in by his best friend or maybe even by one of his parents.

ANYONE CAN DIE

The characters in a dystopian novel are constantly under threat of death and disaster. As a writer, it's important to follow through when you put a character in danger, and sometimes that means giving your readers a shocking turn of events. They won't get as invested in your story if they think there's no chance anything bad could ever befall your protagonist or any other major character. Threats against their lives start to feel hollow.

That is, unless you show them that Anyone Can Die in the world of your novel. Killing off a beloved character proves you mean business. Suddenly the tension in every scene that follows ratchets up. The stakes are alarmingly high. Every threat against your protagonist takes on a sharper edge after an unexpected death. Your readers will be on edge—in a good way—because if you're willing to kill off a major character who they absolutely adored, then they know your protagonist isn't safe either.

If you think of the writer as a god of their narrative domain—after all, the writer is the all-knowing story creator—you have now become a cruel and unjust god. Your readers don't know what you'll do next. Isn't that how you want it?

“Tell Me It’s a Lie”

SCENARIO

There are pockets of light in the darkness. Your protagonist is in an incredible marriage. So, even when she feels despair about the bouts of harsh and chaotic political warfare around them, she always knows she has someone waiting for her at home who proves that goodness is possible. Her husband makes her feel strong and alive. He is the reason she wakes up every morning. He makes her believe it'll all somehow be okay.

BRAINSTORM

Put yourself in your protagonist's head and write her wedding vows. What serious promises did she make to this man? Did she include any playful, silly vows or inside jokes? Don't overthink it, just come up with some romantic, personal, and thoughtful details she would have used in her vows for some insight into the foundation of their marriage. Their emotional bedrock.

WRITE

Your protagonist is home alone performing a simple, quotidian task. Write a scene where she receives word that her husband has been killed in a violent attack perpetrated by the warring government. She doesn't believe the news at first—see how long you can keep her in this state of disbelief. The instant she agrees to accept that this information is real is when she will fall apart. Hold off on that moment. She's not ready to feel that yet.

Remember: Her husband was her rock. He made her feel safe in a scary world. Now that he's gone, who knows what she will become? Who will she turn to for support? In what ways will this change how she navigates her community?

OPTIONAL ELEMENTS TO INCLUDE

- She is denied a viewing of the body.
- Hacked security footage.
- A barcode is tattooed on his neck.

CALLBACKS

What if your protagonist and her husband talked about this possibility? When you live in a world that is so combustible, it's natural to make plans for a tragic situation. What if your protagonist remembers, in her darkest moment, that they each left something behind for each other—a note that the surviving spouse is only allowed to read in the event of their partner's untimely death?

"Promise You'll Do Something for Me"

SCENARIO

Your protagonist is out after curfew with his best friend. He witnesses his friend getting gunned down by officers during a "routine" sweep of the area. They don't bother to kill your protagonist; he just gets a ticket or a stern warning. The random cruelty is a feature of dystopia, not a bug. As your protagonist holds his dying friend, the friend asks him for a favor.

BRAINSTORM

Make a list of oppressive rules the government has told people they must follow at night. Come up with an internal logic for each rule—but make that logic opaque. If people don't understand the rules they're supposed to follow, the government can squeeze the noose even tighter. Imagine that the people who create society's rules think like the officials at the IRS—life would be so confusing, wouldn't it? Capture this tone in the curfew rulebook.

WRITE

Write a scene where your protagonist wants to fulfill what his friend asked of him, but he can't motivate himself to do it. He's horrified that his friend is dead. What he really wants is revenge. But someone else in his life—a mentor character—urges him to complete the deathbed request. There is grace in doing this task for his friend. It may help him find clarity about what he needs to do next.

Remember: Your protagonist and his friend were incredibly close. His friend's absence feels like a lost limb. There might even be moments when he thinks his friend is still there.

OPTIONAL ELEMENTS TO INCLUDE

- ✖ A broken window.
- ✖ An offering of food.
- ✖ A ghost.

CALLBACKS

What if your protagonist keeps seeing his friend where his friend isn't? Could his friend be trying to tell him something from beyond?

"I Didn't Know I'd Never See Him Again"

SCENARIO

Your orphaned protagonist had a rough upbringing—growing up on the streets, always having to dodge officers on patrol. It was a rough-and-tumble existence. When he was a teenager, he got a job (perhaps at a small bakery, blacksmith's shop, or crafts shop). His boss fed him and taught him important things like how to read, becoming both mentor and parent.

BRAINSTORM

Your protagonist knows how his life might have gone if he'd never met his mentor. Envision some of those details. What harsh future did he avoid? Even though the mentor knows her importance, your protagonist has never explicitly expressed gratitude. If he told his mentor everything she means to him, what would he say?

WRITE

Write a quiet scene where your protagonist takes the mentor's help for granted; maybe they share a brief moment together before your protagonist leaves for the day. Then write a scene where he discovers the unthinkable happened while he was gone: His mentor was killed by an errant drone.

OPTIONAL ELEMENTS TO INCLUDE

Broken eyeglasses, an unfinished note, or a disguise.

DYSTOPIAN TWIST

What if the drone wasn't out of control? What if the mentor was targeted? What potentially dangerous information might she have had that someone would silence her for?

Quick Writes

Set a timer for 15 minutes and do not stop writing until the timer goes off. Do not edit, cross out, or censor yourself. Write down every thought that comes to you.

1. What if your protagonist's lover trusted the wrong person? Write a scene where she performs a good deed for someone who hates your protagonist, and this act of kindness leads to her untimely demise.
2. Your protagonist is very close to her family. What would happen if one of her parents attended a protest that got out of control, and they never came home? How would that motivate your protagonist? Write a scene where she learns of her parent's death.
3. Write a scene where your protagonist unexpectedly dies while he is Behind Enemy Lines. Think of which character would be most impacted by this loss and shift your narrative focus to that new character.
4. Your protagonist's best friend tries to stay out of trouble, but your protagonist motivates him to get more involved. Write a scene where they sneak into a government figure's home to steal war plans, and your protagonist watches as his friend is killed by a security guard (or by the government official).
5. Write a scene where your protagonist encounters a very powerful oppressive figure and ends up killing him in self-defense. Unfortunately, no one will ever believe that your protagonist was defending herself. How will she get out of this?

MEDIA EXPLOITATION

In your dystopian novel, there may be no rules about exploiting someone's image. Or maybe your protagonist's face and voice were used in advertisements without his consent. Perhaps he was the subject of a documentary and didn't even know. Once upon a time, Media Exploitation was something only public figures and celebrities worried about, but now everyone's fair game.

What would your protagonist do if he found out his image was manipulated to make it look like he endorsed a politician he despised? How would he react if his smiling face was plastered on a billboard promoting a company whose values he finds reprehensible? What if he saw himself in a commercial for a harmful product he'd never use? What would he do?

Your protagonist's bitter ex might create a deepfake version of him who stars in adult films. The coworker he's competing against for a promotion could release a video that makes it look like he's spewing hateful rhetoric. An estranged friend could create a TV show about their relationship, using your protagonist's name, his image, and a litany of personal details—exposing all his "secrets" (even if they aren't true).

The scariest thing about Media Exploitation is that all these things could happen without your protagonist's knowledge. And when he finds out, his life won't ever be the same.

"I'm Not Your Entertainment!"

SCENARIO

Your protagonist has a meltdown in public that gets caught by surveillance cameras. Soon it's being publicly broadcast. Someone behind the cameras thinks she has "star quality" so they begin airing footage of her whenever she gets caught by their cameras. She doesn't know what's happening at first—then her phone starts blowing up with texts telling her: She's famous now.

BRAINSTORM

What if entertainment as we know it doesn't exist anymore? Think about how celebrity culture might look in a post-movie, post-TV, post-Internet world. When everyone is fair game, it benefits you to invade other people's privacy before they can invade yours. So, what is it about your protagonist that makes people want to keep watching her every move? What are her most arresting qualities?

WRITE

Write a scene where your protagonist has another public meltdown, but this time it's directed at the cameras. She hates being watched all the time—it's making her feel insecure and paranoid. Unfortunately, the more she fights against her fame, the more people want to watch her. And cameras are everywhere, so she'll have to be clever if she wants to avoid them.

Remember: She's an ordinary person. She doesn't have media training. Maybe this is why people can't look away: She's unpredictable and everyone's dying to see what she'll do next. They watch her every move, analyzing her motivations, debating why she did certain things, even making predictions about what she might do next. She has legions of fans and hordes of detractors, and they all want the same thing: more content.

OPTIONAL ELEMENTS TO INCLUDE

- ✖ She gets mugged on camera and no one stops to help.
- ✖ The more famous she gets, the more stalkers she has.
- ✖ She loses her job because her fame's too distracting.

DYSTOPIAN TWIST

What would happen if she staged an "entertainment strike" and refused to do anything that strangers might find interesting? Would people still watch if she sat in front of an electronic billboard watching live footage of herself doing nothing? And when they do finally get bored with her, who will be the next subject of society's poisonous fascination?

"They're All Going to See the Real Me"

SCENARIO

Employee protections are a thing of the past. These days, there aren't enough bodies to do the work due to the plague—so no restrictions are in place and it's completely normal to operate dangerous equipment for long hours. Which is what your protagonist was doing when she fell asleep and injured herself. The new scar on her face will prevent her from ever forgetting what she went through.

BRAINSTORM

How would she react if a shady company used an unauthorized photo of her in an ad campaign? Is she horrified to see her face on a billboard with the scar removed? Or does it give her a thrill?

WRITE

Write a scene where your protagonist does something drastic to get rid of or replace the billboards that feature her face. If her face is going to be out there in the public eye, her physical imperfections should be on display too.

OPTIONAL ELEMENTS TO INCLUDE

- ✖ A press conference.
- ✖ Alcohol.
- ✖ A moment of seduction.

DYSTOPIAN TWIST

What if your protagonist is making too big a deal out of this? What if the shady company does this all the time—one face is the same as the next one? They don't care how she feels. By the time she has her big public scar reveal, the ad with her face on it is already gone.

"Delete That Before I Delete You"

SCENARIO

Your protagonist's brain was hacked by a group of swindlers who threaten to release his most private thoughts unless he gives them money. But he won't let anyone extort him. He might be nice at first, but he ultimately threatens them. If they release or share his private thoughts with anyone, he will make it his personal mission to see that everyone involved in this scheme is physically, emotionally, and financially destroyed.

BRAINSTORM

What is your protagonist hiding? Make a list of at least ten thoughts he wouldn't want anyone else to know. Let his thoughts be a stream of consciousness. These chaotic thoughts aren't meant for public consumption.

WRITE

Write a scene where your protagonist tracks down one of the brain hackers and gives him a message to pass on to his accomplices. He wants them to know he means business—so instead of using words, he delivers his message with violence. Show how their actions have driven him to the edge of his sanity. He doesn't realize how carried away he's gotten until it's too late to stop.

Remember: This might be totally out of character for your protagonist. Maybe he's never threatened anyone before. Perhaps he doesn't even recognize himself right now. But he will go to extremes to protect his private thoughts. No one should endure that kind of violation.

OPTIONAL ELEMENTS TO INCLUDE

- ✖ A sudden, intense headache that floors your protagonist.
- ✖ The hackers have downloaded images from his memory.
- ✖ He suspects this wasn't a random attack.

CALLBACKS

Consider the idea that your protagonist has a skeleton in his closet that he thought he had buried forever. He did something bad, but he's atoned for his actions. Now he wants to move on. What are the chances these criminals will let him?

Quick Writes

Set a timer for 15 minutes and do not stop writing until the timer goes off. Do not edit, cross out, or censor yourself. Write down every thought that comes to you.

1. Write a scene where your protagonist finds out his doctor sold his medical records to a publishing company. The X-rays from his hernia surgery will be in a coffee table book.
2. Write a scene where your protagonist sees a deepfake version of himself assassinating a world leader on live TV. Will anyone believe it wasn't really him?
3. Write a scene where your protagonist discovers her likeness is being used on a trashy reality show that isn't real. Even though her AI counterpart is a terrible person, everyone assumes the worst and blames your protagonist.
4. Your protagonist is a minor celebrity. People trust him. But then he sees an ad on TV where he appears to be endorsing an evil politician. What the hell?
5. Your protagonist isn't being exploited by the media—her child is. Write a scene where she goes on a full "mama bear" rampage, trying to find out who's responsible for this violation.

CHILDREN ARE OBSOLETE

Imagine how rich you'd be if you could invest in a stock that goes up every time a parent worries. Those worries skyrocket when you live in a world where even babies face the threat of deportation simply because of their genetic makeup.

There's no place for a loving parent-child relationship in a world where Children Are Obsolete. You might live in fear that a regime will assume your parental responsibilities just because they feel like it. Or laws might be enacted that require mandatory sterility to prevent overpopulation. Or menstrual cycles might be monitored by federal agencies to ensure only the "right" person has kids. Or birth control might require a permit, even though unwanted pregnancies have been made illegal.

There are many reasons why those in power target kids. A strictly regimented society views the laughter of little ones, wonder, and play as unnecessary indulgences. Children take up too much space, too many resources, too much energy. Caring for them is a distraction for adults who should be focused on jobs that demand long workdays in service of the government.

And yet, people persist. Your protagonist might be on a mission to have children despite it all, or to keep his children from being kidnapped by authorities, or to discover where a child's been taken and how to get her back. These can be the darkest dystopian stories, but when your protagonist succeeds, victory is sweet. Your readers will pull for him all the way.

"The Only Thing That Keeps Me Alive Is Knowing She's Out There"

SCENARIO

There are no more children in the world of your story. They've either been outlawed, eliminated (if you want to go that dark), or taken away to an unknown location for an unknown fate. Many people are in mourning, but they keep their feelings to themselves. It's safer that way.

BRAINSTORM

Think about what may have happened to these children. Think about where they've been taken and how hard it is for them to communicate with the outside world. Come up with three different ways they might try—and rank the methods from least to most dangerous.

WRITE

Write a scene where your protagonist receives a covert message indicating that her child is alive and well. Your protagonist cannot celebrate—to create a scene or focus attention on herself would only put her child at greater risk. But she is screaming with joy on the inside. Who does she confide in? Think of all the ways this news gives her strength to carry on.

OPTIONAL ELEMENTS TO INCLUDE

- ✖ A fingerprint.
- ✖ A portion of the message has been destroyed or smudged.
- ✖ Your protagonist must pay for the message (either with money they don't have or a favor that will be difficult to accomplish).

DYSTOPIAN TWIST

What if your protagonist accidentally received a message intended for someone else? Another child's letter to a different home. Either she doesn't realize it wasn't meant for her, or she knows and doesn't care. False hope is still hope, isn't it?

CALLBACKS

Parents and children have code words, inside jokes, private memories. What if your protagonist's child included a secret code in their message? A reference to a moment from their shared past that only your protagonist would understand.

“I’m Doing It for Our Future”

SCENARIO

It’s illegal for humans to give birth. All children are now conceived in labs, where they go through the entire gestation process and every step of early development is regulated. The uterus has become an unnecessary organ; this is a time of compulsory sterilization, mandatory hysterectomies, even intercourse bans. And yet, that doesn’t stop people from wanting a family.

BRAINSTORM

You decide what happens to children after they’re born: Are they raised in an institutional setting? Do they go to a “child farm” where their organs will ultimately be harvested? Are they put to work as soon as they can walk? Or does some other unusual and barbaric fate await them?

WRITE

Your protagonist wants a child more than anything. She doesn’t care if it’s illegal and she’s not going to listen to the rich, elite, greedy one-percenters in charge. Those ghouls do not get to tell her what she can do with her body. Write a scene where she convinces her partner to ignore the law and secretly have a baby with her.

OPTIONAL ELEMENTS TO INCLUDE

- An ultimatum.
- A pregnancy test purchased on the black market.
- She quotes their wedding vows.

CALLBACKS

What was your protagonist’s stance on having children when she first met her spouse? How have her feelings evolved over the course of their relationship? In an effort to change her mind now, her spouse quotes something she said when they first met about not wanting kids.

"They Can't Find Out She Has a Twin"

SCENARIO

Your protagonist is in the middle of a political maelstrom. His child was taken from him by a powerful government agency and shipped off to another country. This traumatic event thrust your protagonist into the international spotlight, even though these abductions are becoming more and more frequent. Over time, he becomes a spokesperson for issues such as immigration reform and basic human rights. But people are noticing he gets cagey with some of his answers. Why does he always dodge certain questions about his personal life?

BRAINSTORM

Come up with a list of hard-hitting questions for your protagonist, as if you were a reporter. Try to get your protagonist to slip up and say something he shouldn't say. What questions does he get again and again? What questions does he hate? What's the one question no one has asked him that would unsettle him the most?

WRITE

Write a scene where your protagonist and his spouse have a quiet moment together and talk about the secret whereabouts of their child. Not the child who was taken—their other child. The one no one knows about. The one they're hiding. They will do whatever it takes—blackmail, murder, terrorism, anything—to protect their secret kid.

Remember: Your protagonist and his spouse aren't the only ones who know about this child. How many people are they depending on to stay silent?

OPTIONAL ELEMENTS TO INCLUDE

- ✖ Poison.
- ✖ A hidden door.
- ✖ A nagging cough.

DYSTOPIAN TWIST

Why would the government take an innocent child and separate them from their family? Think about how cold and heartless someone would have to be to approve of this action. Now that your protagonist is in the public eye, he's meeting all sorts of people—including people who think the government was justified. What kind of world is this? How does your protagonist respond to this extremism?

Quick Writes

Set a timer for 15 minutes and do not stop writing until the timer goes off. Do not edit, cross out, or censor yourself. Write down every thought that comes to you.

1. Write a scene where your protagonist hides her child in an abandoned location and promises to come back. Will she? Can she?
2. Your protagonist discovers a child on her doorstep. It would be insane to take the child in. But this innocent young person needs her help. Write a scene where she feeds the child and asks a trusted confidante for advice.
3. Your pregnant protagonist needs to get out of the country before she starts showing. Write a scene where a border control agent takes her into a small room for questioning.
4. Your protagonist discovers his child was taken in the middle of the night. His spouse is missing too. Write a scene where he frantically searches for clues.
5. Write a scene where your protagonist makes coffee for a military officer who has unexpectedly shown up for a home inspection. Your protagonist's children are hiding in the attic or basement. Will they get caught?

SECRET SELF-EXPRESSION

Visualize a world without artistic expression. Music is illegal; you can't sing, play an instrument, or listen to a recording. Painting is illegal; the museums are gone, and all the great pieces of art have been destroyed. Creative writing is illegal; there are no more movies, plays, books, or poems. Taking photographs for anything other than surveillance purposes is strictly forbidden. Dancing is a crime; it isn't just performances that are illegal, but dancing for fun is out of the question as well. The only artwork deemed acceptable by the government is soulless AI-created drivel.

Wouldn't life be boring if you stripped away all that joy? But this is what a government does when it couldn't care less about its citizens. So-called leaders in this administration see these forms of expression as dangerous because they encourage thinking and empathy, and, well, the fact is they can control the masses better when people think and empathize less.

But all this oppression doesn't annihilate the arts. It just pushes the artists underground. Musicians, painters, writers, photographers, dancers, and other artistic types are driven by inner forces that can't be suppressed by outsiders. The creative spirit is remarkably resilient. Art will find a way—through Secret Self-Expression.

"Everyone Will Know Your Words"

SCENARIO

Your protagonist has a mentor who helped her become the person she is today. He invited her into his secret library where he taught her how to read—an act that has long been forbidden within their city walls. He showed her a world with hope in it, taught her determination, and through his books, helped her experience joy for the first time. Thanks to his teachings, she knows how much words matter.

BRAINSTORM

The mentor has lost a lot in his lifetime—but he has been given many gifts as well. Examine how his life has been enriched by teaching your protagonist.

WRITE

Write a deathbed scene for the mentor where your protagonist promises to publish everything he wrote. She will do whatever it takes; she'll break the law, she'll steal the supplies, she'll distribute his work door-to-door if she must. It's a travesty that he's been silenced for so long. She will make it her duty to bring his voice to the people.

Remember: They have been through a lot together. He has kept her safe. He knows she can protect herself now but still worries about her. Whatever she says to him during their last moments will quell any fears he has.

OPTIONAL ELEMENTS TO INCLUDE

- ✖ A poem.
- ✖ A song.
- ✖ A blood oath.

DYSTOPIAN TWIST

What if this isn't a death by natural causes? What if the mentor was targeted because of his art? Now that he's gone, your protagonist could be a target too. His words are too dangerous. And someone out there is determined to destroy them.

CALLBACKS

Think about the beginning of their relationship. What was the first piece of writing he shared with her? Perhaps she quotes him now to show how deeply his writing has affected her. No matter what, she will always have his words.

"Give a Copy of This Poem to Every Person You See"

SCENARIO

Your protagonist is reading a government-sponsored textbook at the library. All libraries countrywide have a limited number of books—only those sanctioned by the authorities. As your protagonist turns the pages, a slip of paper falls out. It's a poem.

BRAINSTORM

Imagine the rush of energy pulsing through his body as he reads this poem. It's the first time he's read anything artistic. How does it feel to find yourself entering a new world through words?

WRITE

Write a scene where your protagonist secretly makes a hundred copies of this poem. (Maybe he has to write them by hand!) He asks a close friend to help distribute this small piece of beauty.

OPTIONAL ELEMENTS TO INCLUDE

- ✖ An angry old man.
- ✖ A sense of hope.
- ✖ A smoggy sky.

DYSTOPIAN TWIST

What if the friend destroys all the poems? It isn't a malicious act—he's just being protective. Because if the wrong person found out about this, there would be dire consequences.

“I Never Dared Hope It Could Feel This Good”

SCENARIO

It's been so long since art existed that some people think it's just a strange rumor from the past. It was all destroyed during a brutal censorship war. The only people who've experienced things like books, music, and painting are the elderly. Younger people have heard the rumors, but most smile and nod: "Nice story about the past, Grandma."

BRAINSTORM

There's something in your protagonist—an impulse, a deep desire—that makes her feel alien and alone. She has a need to express herself, but she's never been given a way to do it. Think about how it would feel to know you are an artist but not have the language to express your art. How does a soul express itself without any tools?

WRITE

Write a scene where your protagonist clears out an old storage unit or warehouse and discovers a treasure trove of art supplies. She doesn't know where to start. How do you even use paint? What is this stick with bristles on the end of it? But she slowly figures it out. And as she paints, she discovers who she is. It's like putting a key into a lock and opening the door.

Remember: Your protagonist was driven to this. On another day, she might have tossed out the art supplies without looking at them. What is it about this day that inspired her to experiment?

OPTIONAL ELEMENTS TO INCLUDE

- The color chartreuse.
- Messiness.
- She paints with her hands.

DYSTOPIAN TWIST

What if someone spies on her while she creates her first piece of art? Is he angry, curious, jealous, afraid, turned on? What if he has artistic desire too, but he's buried it so deep that he'll never access it again. Think about what this kind of suppression does to a person. He doesn't have the ability to let his own light shine—will he extinguish hers?

Quick Writes

Set a timer for 15 minutes and do not stop writing until the timer goes off. Do not edit, cross out, or censor yourself. Write down every thought that comes to you.

1. Your protagonist has been working on a meaningful visual project in secret. Write a scene where she finally shows it to someone, and they don't react the way she expected.
2. Write a scene where your protagonist disrupts an impending execution by leading a group of singers in a choral chant. Can they get others to join in? Can they stop the execution?
3. Your protagonist meets a stranger and discovers they both secretly practice art. Write a scene where the stranger invites him to an underground club where people are free to express themselves.
4. Your protagonist knows someone who used to play a musical instrument. Write a scene where he begs for a lesson. He doesn't care how dangerous it is; he needs to make music.
5. Write a scene where your protagonist vandalizes a government building with a poem. How long does it take for officials to paint over it, and how do people react in the meantime?